COPING WITH

Drug Abuse

GABRIELLE I. EDWARDS

Illustrated by Nancy Lou Gahan

THE ROSEN PUBLISHING GROUP, INC./NEW YORK

52251

Published in 1983, 1988, 1990 by The Rosen Publishing Group, Inc.
29 East 21st Street, New York, N.Y. 10010

Copyright 1983, 1988, 1990 by Gabrielle I. Edwards

Revised Edition 1990

Library of Congress Cataloging in Publication Data
Edwards, Gabrielle I.
 Coping with drug abuse.

 93-18588

 (Coping)
 Includes index
 Bibliography: p. 161
 1. Drug abuse–Physiological aspects.
2. Psychotropic drugs–Physiological effect.
I. Title.   II. Series: Coping (Rosen Publishing Group)
RC564.E34   1983   613.8'3   83-3341
ISBN 0-8239-1144-6

Manufactured in the United States of America

ABOUT THE AUTHOR ◇

Mrs. Gabrielle I. Edwards was formerly Assistant Principal Supervision of the Science Department at Franklin D. Roosevelt High School in Brooklyn. Although her principal subject areas were biology and general science, she supervised chemistry, physics, earth science, laboratory techniques, medical laboratory assisting, advanced placement biology, and psychobiology.

The holder of bachelor's and master's degrees in biology, general science, and education from Brooklyn College, Mrs. Edwards taught for thirty-eight years in the New York City school system. After serving as a teacher of general science for four years, Mrs. Edwards was appointed to the senior high school, where she remained for thirty years. For twenty-three years she was the supervisor of a large and active science department.

Mrs. Edwards is the author of several books for students in junior and senior high school, including *Coping with Discrimination, Coping with Venereal Disease, Biology the Easy Way, and Living Things* (co-authored).

Her professional affiliations include active membership in the Biology Chairmen's Association, the New York Biology Teachers Association, the Science Council of New

York, the National Association of Biology Teachers, the National Science Teachers Association, and the New York State Science Supervisors' Association.

Because of her numerous and useful contributions to education, Mrs. Edwards recently was the recipient of two prestigious awards. The first of these was presented by the Board of Education of the City of New York in recognition of her outstanding performance in supervision. The second award was a national one. Mrs. Edwards was selected by the National Science Teachers Association as the Outstanding Science Supervisor of the nation for her substantive contributions to the field of science education.

Although having recently retired from the school system, Gabrielle Edwards maintains professional activity in education. She serves on the New York State Commission for Equity in Science for Women and Minorities. She is also the Executive Director for St. Mary's Community Services, an outreach organization that prepares educational programs in the prevention of substance abuse for teenagers and young adults.

Contents

Preface

A person's life is like a pentagon: a five-sided figure. Each side faces its own direction and experiences varying life forces. We can identify these forces: sociological, educational, psychological, economic, and biological. Each life force contributes to the whole individual, giving depth and direction to a person's existence. Drug abuse touches and changes the many sides of a person's life.

Each one of us has a niche in society. A niche means more than a place to live. It means personal involvement with others. We have a relationship with family, friends, schoolmates or work associates, and people of the community in which we live. We adjust ourselves to fit in with all of these social situations. This is the sociological niche. Misuse of drugs invariably alters and destroys our relations with others.

In our society, a young person is expected to spend at least twelve years of his life in school. During this time he or she learns to read, to express himself (herself) in writing, and to use skills of mathematics. He is also exposed to areas of learning that involve higher academic skills and vocational knowledge. The length and direction of a person's education is abruptly shortened when he becomes seriously involved with drugs. There is no question that drugs affect a person's educational life.

Adults have daily obligations in work situations or at home. When earning a living, a person is expected to report to work each day and to be there on time. It is expected that each worker do his best at the job for which he is being paid. A person who remains home to take care of the family must function well in order to raise children properly and to provide the best possible emotional environment for the family. Adult drug users hurt themselves and their families even more.

As human beings we must respond to and adjust to the changing situations of life. It is not unreasonable to expect that sometimes we will be happy, at other times sad. We experience periods of frustration, anxiety, boredom, calm, giddiness, anger, and so forth. These are our emotions at work. Every person has emotional needs, feelings that must be satisfied. Most people find constructive outlets for their emotions. Hobbies, sports, work, and helping others are some ways that can be used to help us maintain positive behavior patterns. But the person committed to the use of drugs is hard pressed to control his human drives by himself. He is drug-dependent, and therefore his psychological life is chemically controlled.

Drug abusers can be of any age. Many older people are caught in a cycle of drug abuse. They take drugs to lift their moods, make them sleep, and calm their "nerves." They take one drug to counteract the effect of another. Sometimes drug-taking alters their ability to hold a job or to progress in their life's work. In addition, the cost of a drug habit is exorbitant. It is not difficult to understand that drugs affect people economically.

A number of young professionals, highly skilled and seemingly successful in the world of business, have joined the ranks of drug abusers. Although this group has excelled in the competitive workplace and reached the top of the financial heap, something goes wrong. They turn to drugs, possibly for relief from stress. Perhaps the demands of their work leave them little time for relaxation with family and friends. Or, because they have struggled so hard to reach the top of their profession, they panic at the idea of being replaced by someone younger and brighter. Feelings of conflict, fear, and loneliness may be the vehicle that delivers these young professionals into the hands of drug dealers.

Although all of the parts that make up a person's life are important, the purpose of this book is to provide information about the biology of drug abuse. What happens when a person takes a drug into his body? Where does it go? What effect does it have? How does it leave the body? Is there permanent damage to the body organs? How do we cope with drug abuse?

As you probably know, the body is made up of billions of cells. Each cell carries out life processes that are necessary to the proper functioning of the whole body. Most cells are not independent. Groups of similar cells work together to form tissues. Various types of tissues form organs. Organs are grouped into systems, which coordinate the activities necessary for life. You have many systems: the nervous, the circulatory, the digestive, the excretory, the respiratory, and the reproductive. In a healthy body these systems work well, carrying out complex tasks of life.

It is the aim of this book to present you with some important facts of drug abuse. You will learn what a particular drug is, where it is obtained, and how it affects the body. It is hoped that these chapters will give you a clear, unbiased picture of what the drug scene is really like.

CHAPTER 1

Medicines

Versus Drugs

What is meant by the word "drug"? According to the dictionary, a drug is "any substance, other than food, intended for use in diagnosis, cure, mitigation, treatment, or prevention of disease in man or other animals." This is a rather involved definition that can be made clearer by the following example:

Willie gets sick. In addition to high body temperature, he has muscular aches, a painful cough, and a general feeling of bodily distress. On the basis of tests, the doctor diagnoses the illness as pneumonia, caused by bacterial infection in his lungs. The toxins (poisons) of the invading germs have caused Willie's illness. The doctor prescribes an antibiotic drug that will stop the growth of bacteria in Willie's lungs without causing harm to his body tissues. Willie is told to take the medicine for seven days. He must drink plenty of water and stay in bed.

Within a week he feels better; his symptoms of pneumonia have decreased. Shortly thereafter, he is well.

Willie no longer has need of the medicine, nor does he feel the desire to continue taking it. This example points out that prescribed drugs are useful in ridding the body of infectious organisms and restoring the person to health. We shall refer to such drugs as medicines.

The characteristics of medicines are as follows:

1. Most are taken on a short-term basis. Once used for a specific purpose to diagnose, treat, lessen, or cure a condition, they are no longer necessary.
2. Some medicines have to be taken for long periods of time, even for a lifetime. A hormone such as insulin is necessary for the life of the diabetic because it enables the body cells to metabolize sugar.
3. A person may stop taking a medicine at will with no craving or pangs of withdrawal. There may be other effects such as those that diabetics experience when they forget to take the daily required dosage of insulin.

We can now understand that the class of drugs referred to as medicines are useful and necessary at times during our lives.

THE ABUSED DRUGS

Unlike medicines, abused drugs are not taken to cure physical ailments. That is why this group of drugs is said to be called "abused." They are taken for reasons that may not even be known to the user.

Pharmacologists, scientists who study drugs, tell us that the chemical actions of drugs change the structure and function of living cells, especially those of the central nervous system. Tampering with normal cellular processes often leads to mental upset, physical disorder, and emotional dependency. In reality, drug abuse causes harm to the body, because most of these chemicals are mood changers that alter normal behavior.

From the late 1960s through the middle '70s methamphetamine was known in the streets as "speed." It is a violent mood changer. (As you read Chapter 3, you will learn more about the amphetamines, the family to which methamphetamine belongs.) "Speed freaks" were often recognizable by the open running sores on their faces and arms, which resulted from picking or digging out imaginary "crank" bugs. In the words of a user:

"It's just that when you're shooting speed constantly you start to feel like there's bugs going around under your skin and you know they're not there, but you pick at them anyway. You go through all these changes scratching. Once in a while you'll see a little black spot and you'll watch it for ten minutes to see if it moves. If it doesn't move it isn't alive. You can feel them on your skin. I'm always trying to pick them out of my eyebrows."

Hallucinations were just one symptom of the paranoia that troubled "speed freaks." Feeling that someone was always after them, they would misinterpret simple statements and innocent actions of strangers and friends alike. It was not unusual for them to become violent psychotics whose severe depression drove them to murder or suicide. Thus a popular slogan became "speed kills."

Currently a problem that has become epidemic is child abuse. A very large percentage of abusing parents are involved with drugs, usually alcohol, heroin, ampheta-

Some young people wear
stickpin buttons that carry a
short, powerful message.

mines, or crack. These words were written by a first-term
high school student:

> "I hate to go home in the afternoon so I just walk
> around the streets. If my mother is not drunk she is
> ok. But when she is bombed, she sometimes beats me
> like she wants to kill me."

After months of trying, the school guidance counselor
was finally successful in getting Alice's mother to come
to school for a conference on the youngster's progress.
During the course of the discussion, Alice jumped up
shouting:

> "Ask her how I got these scars and cuts on my body.
> When I was little, she and her boyfriend would get
> stoned on pills. Then they would take turns beating
> me and burning me just for kicks. If she comes near
> me again, I'll kill her."

A BIT OF TERMINOLOGY

Sometimes the seriousness of drug abuse is hidden in terminology. It is quite common to hear people describe drug-taking in terms of "kicks," "jag," "mind expanding," "turning on," "turning in," "high," or "controlling one's head." These are kind of fun terms, which have become part of the vocabulary of even the nonuser. They tend to mask the real implications of drug involvement.

On the other hand, at times we are bombarded with harsher terms such as "illegal drugs," "illicit drugs," "abused drugs," "misused drugs," "addictive drugs," and the like. These descriptions remind us that drug-taking is a serious business. But what do these words mean? Illegal and illicit mean the same thing. An illegal drug is one that is not permitted to be manufactured or sold. The manufacture and sale of amphetamines and barbiturates is legal under the conditions prescribed by law. When people take these drugs excessively to get intoxicated, the situation is described as drug abuse. The drugs become known as "abused drugs." At times a physician prescribes certain drugs in a given dosage to correct a condition. The patient, liking the effects of the drug, begins to misuse the medication. The World Health Organization emphasizes that all drugs, if misused, cause detrimental effects, which may result in the breakdown of body cells or the death of the person.

THE PILL STORY

We live in a pill-minded society where pills are a way of life. Keep a record of the kinds of pills that are advertised on television. Note that high-pressure salesmen-actors invite you to consume pills to fight the "minor ailments" of colds, headache, heartburn, backache, muscle soreness, hay fever, itching, stomach upset, sleeplessness, nervous tension, liver disorders, vitamin deficiencies, and so forth and so on. There is no end to the variety of pills that are offered for self-treatment.

Pills that can be purchased without a doctor's prescription are called patent medicines. They contain ingredients that usually are not harmful to the average person if the medicine is taken as directed. However, not all types of pills can be purchased at will. Some are sold only to persons who have a prescription from a licensed doctor. Whether pills are patent or prescribed, Americans swallow innumerable tons of them each year.

Pill manufacture is big business. Pharmaceutical houses compound pills of all sizes, shapes, and colors. Pills are manufactured to meet the varying needs of the population. Unlike the haphazard production of angel dust and marijuana joints, pill manufacture is controlled by reputable firms, which invest a great deal of money and effort into compounding medicines that are uniformly reliable in chemical content, weight, purity, and stability.

Teams of research chemists, biochemists, and pharmacologists work out formulas for medicines by using scientific methods and up-to-date machinery. Each kind of tablet, powder, and capsule has to pass rigid standards for safety, quality, and reliability before being released for public use. Under conditions of rigid government control, drug companies turn out products of reliable quality.

DESIGNER DRUGS

While reputable pharmaceutical houses strive for quality in the manufacture of medicines, unprincipled chemists strive to make drugs that will bring them high profits on

tetrahydrocannabinol. This name is commonly shortened to THC. More than thirty cannabinoids have been isolated from marijuana. Many of them are inactive, producing no effect in animals or human beings. Others of the cannabinoids are chemically active. In addition to THC, some of the other important cannabinoids are cannabichromene (CBC), cannabinol (CBN), and cannabidiol (CBD).

Marijuana is a very strange plant. Its chemical composition changes according to the region in which it is grown. Marijuana grown in Colombia contains very potent THC capable of inducing hallucinations in first-time users. Jamaican Cannabis contains a milder form of THC that differs from the Mexican variety. Only within very recent years have research workers been able to ascertain the exact strength and chemical composition of the marijuana they were growing for use in experiments. Not only does the strength of the THC and the amounts of other cannabinoids vary with the geography of the plant, but also different parts of the plant contain different amounts of the active compounds. The leaves of Cannabis might contain only 1 or 2 percent of THC while the flowering bracts may contain 10 percent or more. Also, the THC content in the same plant may vary greatly from morning to evening.

HOW MARIJUANA WORKS IN THE BODY

The dried leaves of Cannabis are ground up and rolled into crude cigarettes called "reefers" or "joints." A "roach" refers to a partially smoked joint. The THC is taken into the body by smoking marijuana with slow deep inhalations. It takes about ten minutes for the smoker to get the effect, a "high" that lasts for about three hours.

When a joint of marijuana is smoked, where does the active THC go? First of all, THC is carried by the bloodstream to the brain. Its effect on the brain's medulla and the reticular formation results in the feeling of intoxication that the smoker wants. Dr. Julius Axelrod, one of the Nobel laureates in medicine and physiology in 1970, and a team of researcher workers found out what happens in body cells after the "high" wears off. THC remains in the blood in its active state for more than three days. Some of the THC seeps into the lungs, the brain, and the liver. The liver changes THC into a compound that may be even more potent than delta 9-tetrahydrocannabinol. The chemical breakdown products formed in the liver remain in the body for more than eight days. THC and its breakdown products are not water-soluble. This means that they do not dissolve in water and do not filter out readily through the kidney tubules.

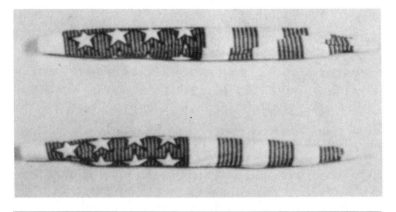

COURTESY CAROLINA BIOLOGICAL SUPPLY COMPANY
The ground leaves of marijuana are rolled into a joint.

THC is extremely soluble in fats, as are its breakdown products. As these compounds diffuse into body cells, they dissolve in the fat molecules of cell membranes and in fatty tissues. It is believed that the fat-soluble cannabinoids may prevent some proteins from entering the cells. Research workers have incorporated radioactive carbon into delta 9-THC. They have thus been able to trace the pathway of this compound through the body. This research has revealed that THC and its metabolites dissolve in the fatty tissues of the brain, gonads, and adrenal glands, where they remain from three to thirty days. The human body absorbs THC very readily. The drug diffuses into body cells so completely that less than 1 percent is eliminated in body wastes. It is believed that the body's ready absorption of THC and the slow rate at which it is eliminated may cause reverse tolerance in frequent users: they can use less of the drug to get its effects.

NEW CLINICAL EVIDENCE AGAINST MARIJUANA

As the research evidence against marijuana increases, arguments in its favor become less strong. A few years ago there seemed to be movement toward the decriminalization of possession of small amounts of the weed. Currently, liberal views toward marijuana use seem not to be expressed so frequently or so forcefully. Now a bit of caution has crept into the political support of marijuana. A growing body of research scientists insists that there is strong evidence that Cannabis is not only a hazard to health but may be more dangerous than some of the so-called hard drugs.

A case in point follows: In October 1982 research workers at Boston University Medical School reported their findings on children born of mothers who smoke marijuana during pregnancy. These children have smaller body weight and are of smaller size than children born to non-marijuana-smoking mothers. It has been noted that these small "marijuana" babies have tendencies toward other abnormalities such as heart defects and slightly distorted facial and other features.

Dr. Philip Zeidenberg, senior research psychiatrist, Department of Biological Psychiatry, New York State Psychiatric Institute, and research associate in psychiatry, Columbia University College of Physicians and Surgeons, notes some toxic effects of Cannabis. "Chronic marijuana-smoking causes bronchitis, diminished lung capacity, and abnormal microscopic changes in lung tissue. In the long run, chronic marijuana-smoking may have many of the lung effects of tobacco." Regarding the effect of marijuana on behavior, Dr. Zeidenberg notes, "There is no doubt that a single dose of THC can cause an acute psychotic reaction in mentally healthy people." Marijuana use is also associated with longer-lasting and even chronic psychoses. Many of these people, but not all, are found to have a previous history of serious mental illness.

Dr. Cecile Leuchtenberger, head of cytochemistry, Swiss Institute for Experimental Cancer Research, Lausanne, states: "The observations that marijuana cigarette smoke stimulates irregular growth in the respiratory system, that it interferes with DNA stability of cells and of chromosomes, that it disturbs the genetic equilibrium, strongly suggest that marijuana cigarette smoke is a health hazard which may not only be implicated in lung carcinogenesis, but may also have mutagenic potentialities."

In a recent issue of the *Journal* of the American Medical Association, Dr. Harold Kolansky and Dr. William T. Moore of the Department of Psychiatry, University of Pennsylvania, and the Institute of the Philadelphia Association for Psychoanalysis wrote:

"After seven years of clinical observation, we have become concerned that marijuana use adversely affects cerebral functioning on a biochemical basis. In the mildest cases there appears to be a temporary toxic reaction when small amounts of Cannabis are consumed over a short period of time. However, in those individuals who demonstrate stereotyped symptomatology after prolonged and intensive Cannabis use, the possibility of structural changes in the cerebral cortex must be raised."

In simple terms these investigators are saying that there is some evidence that it is possible for marijuana to cause physical brain damage.

Other researchers concur. Dr. A.M.G. Campbell of the Department of Neurology at Britain's Bristol Royal United Hospital reported that death of brain cells was clearly demonstrated by a process known as air encephalography in ten patients with histories of consistent marijuana smoking over a period of time ranging from three to eleven years. Dr. Hardin B. Jones, professor of medical physics and physiology at the University of California, says that marijuana brings about brain-wave changes and mental dullness. He points out that once marijuana enters the body it accumulates in the brain and leaves it at only 1/100 the rate of its breakdown in the body. This means that the drug may remain in the brain of some people for about a year.

There is another side to the marijuana story, as illustrated by the ongoing work of reputable science research workers. Unfortunately a political position may be expedient for vote-getting but may not serve the needs of the health and well-being of a population. Repeated use of marijuana is not as harmless as suggested.

Recent statistics reveal that an estimated four million juveniles aged twelve to seventeen currently use marijuana. These child smokers are absorbing poisons from a species of Cannabis that comes from Colombia and is ten times stronger than that used in the 1960s. This stronger Cannabis impairs brain function, distorts perception, and stores itself in vital organs.

Investigators are finding out that marijuana is not a harmless "fun" drug as earlier reported. Dr. Sidney Cohen of the School of Medicine, University of California, Los Angeles, describes a study that established this alarming fact: smoking five marijuana cigarettes a week has the same effect on the lungs are smoking 112 tobacco cigarettes! Tests at UCLA show that impairment of driving ability persists for several hours after the smoker's high has vanished.

Pot is producing a generation of teenage zombies whose sole motivation in life is to smoke marijuana.

"I feel good, just getting high in the morning. But then, after a while, I get real tired and fall asleep in class, and stuff."

These are the words of a twelve-year-old "burnout" who "tokes" a minimum of five marijuana joints a day. His only drive in life is to "cop a buzz," that is, to be high as frequently as possible.

It is now strongly believed that marijuana-smoking does have an effect on the behavior and learning patterns of teenagers. Chronic smokers have been described variously: irritable, hostile, always tired, cares less about everything, shows poor school performance, has drastic mood changes. In addition, regular users of marijuana seem to feel chest pains, have a chronic cough, and have some impairment of near vision.

Dr. Harold Voth, senior psychiatrist and psychoanalyst at the Menninger Foundation in Topeka, Kansas, stated, "...there is one pernicious symptom specifically related to marijuana which seems to be evident in every chronic pot user, youngster or adult. This is the extraordinary refusal to accept the hard scientific evidence about the harmful effects of marijuana. The user will scoff at the evidence; twist it, pervert it, call it "reefer madness"— anything except look it straight in the face."

An even sadder note is that younger and younger children, three- and four-year-olds, are given marijuana to smoke by their pot-smoking parents or older siblings. Recently a social case worker reported that a pot-smoking young couple were making their nine-month-old baby high by blowing marijuana smoke in her face.

The evidence is becoming clearer each day. The harmlessness of marijuana use is a myth that ought to go up in smoke.

PHENCYCLIDINE: A DRUG OF TERROR

On the streets it is known as angel dust, green tea, peace pill, hog, busy bee, cyclone, mist, goon, rocket fuel, crystal, super joint, zombie dust, and elephant tranquilizer. Its chemical name is phencyclidine, abbreviated PCP.

Research pharmacologists developed phencyclidine in the late 1950s for use as an anesthetic in surgery. Permission for testing the drug on human subjects was granted in 1963 by the Food and Drug Administration. Phencyclidine functioned well in the operating room, but the aftermath of the drug was terrible. Patients regained consciousness disoriented, delirious, hallucinating, and depressed. Because of these very serious effects, the FDA withdrew its approval for use with humans. However, phencyclidine was approved for manufacture as an animal anesthetic under the trade name Sernvlan.

Since 1967 phencyclidine has moved out of the research laboratories into the streets. Unscrupulous persons with knowledge of organic chemistry set up clandestine laboratories for the illicit production of the drug. In seriously contaminated forms it reaches the streets, where one out of four drug buys is the now infamous angel dust. It is cheap to make, and the profits are high.

Street level abuse has several patterns, depending upon the form in which the drug is manufactured. In pill or capsule form, PCP is swallowed. As a powder, it is either snorted or sprinkled on marijuana, parsley, or mint leaves and smoked. In liquid form, it is either injected or soaked into marijuana leaves.

Drugs manufactured illicitly have no standard formulation, and therefore their physiological action on human beings cannot be predetermined. The way angel dust works in the body is so unpredictable that the same person may be affected in different ways. Thus it has gained another nickname—heaven and hell.

Dr. Robert L. Dupont, director of the National Institute on Drug Abuse, has called PCP "a drug of terror." Nearly a third of the young patients reporting to drug treatment centers have tried PCP. In low dosages it gives the user a free-floating feeling or numbness, the illusion that the mind has separated from the body.

In large doses or with repeated use, PCP does indeed become a drug of terror. It induces symptoms of schizophrenia, leading to suicide and violence. A user in California picked out a house at random, broke in and killed a baby, and then stabbed its mother repeatedly. A man in

Chicago tore out both his eyes with his bare hands while under the influence of angel dust.

At a time when parents have dropped their guard against marijuana, PCP is considered the most dangerous of the "new" drugs peddled on the streets. Its greatest effect is on the brain. Research scientists have determined that phencyclidine is stored in the fat tissues of the brain, and the rate of its breakdown in the liver is very slow. Therefore some people suffer flashbacks after even one use.

Sally, a fifteen-year-old, is one of those who has suffered severe flashbacks, although she has not touched the drug in months. Her manner is hesitating. She is withdrawn and seems constantly spaced out. She speaks in a whisper and experiences catatonic states.

Brian, a nineteen-year-old, described his hallucinations while under the influence of PCP. "I knew that flies were attacking me." At other times "a bowl of soup smiled at me because I was God." He subsequently stepped off a roof and killed himself.

In addition to hallucinations and flashbacks, the user can experience drowsiness, inability to verbalize, difficulty in thinking, poor concentration, and preoccupation with death. Some common signs of phencyclidine use are reddening of the skin and profuse sweating, involuntary eye movements, loss of feeling of pain, double vision, muscular incoordination, dizziness, nausea, and vomiting. Angel dust, killer, zombie dust, or whatever it is called, is a drug with frightening effects. Young people must be warned against its use.

SOME COMMON HALLUCINOGENIC DRUGS

In 1957 Dr. Humphrey Osmond coined the word *psyche-delic* to describe the bizarre colors that mind-changing drugs bring about in users. Under the influence of hallucinogens, a user may speak of "seeing" sounds and "hearing" colors. The senses of direction, distance, and time become disoriented. Until the hallucinogen wears off, the user is restless and cannot sleep. The hallucinogens are dangerous drugs and should not be abused. Some common hallucinogenic drugs are summarized in the table that follows.

Common Hallucinogenic Drugs

Name	Source	How Taken	Effect
Mescaline	Peyote cactus	Swallowed	Exhilaration, anxiety, gastric upset; 12-hour duration
DMT and DET (Dimethyltriptamine and Diethyltriptamine)	Mexican mushroom *Psilocybe caerulescens*	Swallowed	Euphoria to depression, nausea, vomiting, headache; 6-8-hour duration
Cocaine (also classified as a stimulant and hard narcotic)	Leaves of coca plant	Sniffed	Stimulation, excitement, paranoid psychosis, auditory and visual hallucinations; 4-5 hour duration

Common Hallucinogenic Drugs (contd)

Name	Source	How Taken	Effect
Morning glory seeds	Mexican morning glory plant	Chewed	Passivity and unresponsive- ness, with- drawal, vomiting; duration variable
DOM (STP, 4-methyl-2- 5-dimeth- oxyamphet- amine) tamine)	Synthetic derived from mescaline and amphet- amines	Swallowed	Mild hallucinations, euphoria; street name, STP: serenity, tranquility, peace
MDA and MMDA	Synthetics related to the amphetamines mescaline and DOM	Swallowed but may be snorted in powder form	Hallucinations, sense of well- being
Metham- phetamine	Synthetic	Smoked	Hallucinations, paranoia, violence

LSD—THE PAINTED MADNESS

It was in a research laboratory in Switzerland in May 1943 that Dr. Albert Hoffman accidentally discovered the weird hallucinogenic power of d-lysergic acid diethylamide, LSD for short. Five years earlier he and an associate had chemically synthesized lysergic acid diethylamide tartrate from ergot, a fungus of rye. As he was working with the synthetic chemical, Dr. Hoffman inadvertently ingested some. What happened is best told in Dr. Hoffman's own words:

"I noted with dismay that my environment was under-going progressive change. Everything seemed strange and I had the greatest difficulty in expressing myself.

My visual fields wavered and everything appeared deformed as in a faulty mirror. I was overcome by a fear that I was going crazy. The worst part being that I was clearly aware of my condition."

The discovery of the bizarre mental activity caused by LSD stimulated many research studies on the effects and possible medical uses of the drug. Research psychologists and psychiatrists were trying to find a medical cure for schizophrenia, a mental disorder that alters a person's perception. Ironically, LSD did not remain in the research laboratory. Through the channels of unauthorized experimentation on human subjects by certain college investigators and through the ultimate synthesis of LSD in blackmarket laboratories in the late 1960s–middle '70s it became a drug that was frighteningly misused and abused by young people.

LSD has deceiving physical characteristics. Like water, it is colorless, odorless, and tasteless. There the similarity ends. Unlike water, it has never existed in total volume of more than a few ounces, yet the effect on individuals is fierce. A drop of LSD too small to be seen with a magnifying glass is all that is needed to induce hallucinations.

LSD, "acid" to its users, is dropped onto a sugar cube or put into orange juice. Shortly after ingestion, physical changes occur. The pupils of the eyes dilate, heart palpitations occur, the blood pressure is elevated, and the smooth muscles of internal organs contract. These symptoms are mild at first. In thirty minutes hallucinations in all of their deceptive horror begin and last up to ten hours. This is what is known as a "trip."

What a trip it is: The user initially experiences color intensification. He feels that colors are "brighter than ever." Objects take on a luminous glow. There is a confusion of sense perception so that those under the influence of LSD "hear" colors, "see" sounds, and "feel" thoughts from inanimate objects such as chairs and paintings. There is a loss of time and space awareness during which the person imagines that he is a floating organism. A jumble of mixed and unreal images and feelings may occur. Some users know that their heads are separated from their bodies, or feel that their limbs have become disconnected. At one minute the delusions may be interesting and pleasant; the next, so frightening that the drug taker writhes on the floor in agonizing horror and fear. Size and visual distortions often make an ant seem as large and terrifying as a dinosaur, leaving in the person a tremendous panic.

LSD can drive a normal person into a state of violent insanity. Investigators at the University of California, Los Angeles, described seventy persons who were admitted to the hospital in a seven-month period for adverse reactions to the drug. "In every case, the victim experienced one or more severe reactions such as anxiety, depression, or confusion after the effect of LSD should have worn off. Most hospitalized patients remained for more than a month." LSD is not a "fun" drug. Its effects can be serious and lasting.

The horror of LSD is that users are not in control of themselves. Judgment is lost so that the place in the environment becomes unreal. Users, feeling indestructible, do foolish things. Some attempt to fly, killing themselves in the leap. Others walk into rivers or wander into traffic or set themselves afire. The mood fluctuates so that one may feel happy at one moment and experience extreme depression the next. During a "trip" the mind changes through which a person passes occur simultaneously so that there is

no peace or relaxation. For some the horror lasts about ten
hours. Others never recover. They remain committed in
asylums—minds destroyed.

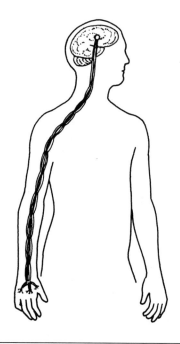

Sensory nerves carry impulses to the brain.

HOW LSD WORKS IN THE BODY

A current research problem is finding out just how LSD
works in body cells and tissues. The National Institute of
Mental Health is using experimental animals to find out
the true nature of immediate and cumulative effects.

Some facts about the physiology of LSD are known.
LSD interferes with the normal activity of brain cells
and tissues. Under normal circumstances, impulses travel
along nerve fibers in orderly sequences. Serotonin, a

neurohumor, is secreted by the axons of sensory neurons. This chemical permits impulses to jump across the synapses from the end brushes of one sensory neuron to the dendrites of another. LSD usurps (steals) the place of serotonin but cannot do the proper job of signal transmission. Therefore, distorted information is sent to the various brain regions.

The medulla of the brain controls reflex and involuntary behavior such as heartbeat, respiration rate, and contraction of smooth muscle. The primary effects of LSD intake indicate that it overstimulates the medulla. Thus a user gets goosebumps on the skin, his eyes redden, the pupils dilate, and his breathing proceeds in short quick gasps. The function of the reticular region in the brain is to sort sensory signals that go to the cerebral cortex for interpreta-

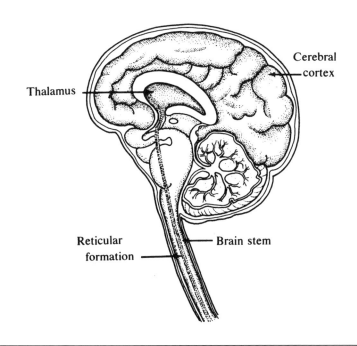

Sections of the brain affected by LSD.

tion. LSD prevents the normal organizing of impulses so that signals transmitted to the cortex are confused. A person therefore "sees" music and "hears" colors. The strange phenomena of undulating walls and floating chairs arise in the thalamus, where abnormally sorted impulses caused by LSD intake are received.

Experimental evidence has indicated that one aspect of LSD use has long-range effects. The breakdown rate in the body can be quite slow. In some people LSD is not broken down completely in the liver. Molecules of the drug seem able to hide within body tissues. At times these seemingly dormant molecules become activated, and the person is "treated" to another LSD trip against his will. This condition is known as a flashback. Why this happens in some people and not in all users is not known.

SUMMARY

The point of this chapter is simple: drugs that cause mind changes are harmful. Hallucinogens are mind-altering because they affect the cells of the involuntary nervous system. This results in abnormal reflex actions and over-stimulation of the brain.

We do not have all the answers concerning marijuana use, but recent research evidence points to the fact that smoking this weed may not be as harmless as believed. THC, the active chemical in marijuana, has a slow breakdown rate in the liver and is stored in fat cells. The effect of this accumulation over a long period of time is unknown.

We do know that phencyclidine (angel dust) is a drug of terror. Because it is stored in the fatty tissue of the brain, flashbacks occur. The effects of use are terrible and frightening.

Also known by the nicknames acid, cubes, trips, Pearly

Gates, and Heavenly Blue, LSD can be quite dangerous to the user. It often leaves the user anxiety-ridden, depressed, and fearful. Months after using the drug, hallucinations may recur in what is called a "flashback." LSD is known to alter the personality for the worse, turning a person who was at one time productive into a dropout from normal society.

CHAPTER 3

The Amphetamines, a Family of Stimulants

A stimulant is a drug that speeds up the metabolic activities of cells of the central nervous system. Some stimulants occur naturally in plants. The caffeine in coffee and the nicotine in tobacco are examples. Others are man-made.

In the 1930s a stimulant of chemical origin was synthesized. This man-made stimulant, named amphetamine, became a base upon which other synthetic stimulants were built. Today the family of amphetamines has grown. At least fifty-seven types of pills are created from this molecule.

FROM RESEARCH TO USE

The original intent in developing the amphetamines was a good one. Drugs that are capable of stimulating the central nervous system have potential use in the treatment of mental disorders. It was found that the amphetamines have value in softening the symptoms of narcolepsy. A person afflicted with this disorder suffers from chronic drowsiness. He cannot carry on the normal doings of life such as working, eating, planning, dancing, thinking. When awake, he is in a state of extreme mental depression, which prevents his functioning. He must be hospitalized. Under the care of a doctor, narcoleptics are helped by administration of amphetamine medication. The disease is not cured, but the patient is able to respond to some of life's drives.

Another type of mental disturbance that responds to amphetamine treatment is hyperactivity in children. As a result of slight brain damage, some children are so overactive that they cannot be handled in a normal group or home situation. Through some biochemical mechanism that is not fully understood, amphetamines do calm hyperactive children temporarily.

As the amphetamine story unfolds, we shall see how these drugs moved out of the hands of the mental hospital clinician into the hands of the general public. A case in point follows. The common cold is a nuisance. Stuffy nostrils cause discomfort that one would rather do without. It was therefore considered quite a boon to medical science and to the drug companies when it was found that a member of the amphetamine family had the ability to shrink nasal membranes. And so Benzedrine was put into nasal sprays and inhalers. Years later, the misuse potential of Benzedrine inhalers was recognized. Now other drugs are being used to relieve stuffy sinuses.

FROM USE TO MISUSE

Today's market in the manufacture and sale of amphetamine drugs has mushroomed. The amphetamine boom could not have been predicted thirty-five years ago. It is estimated that for every man, woman, and child in the United States, seventy amphetamine-based pills are manufactured per year. The legitimate domestic market nets about $54 million a year from sale of amphetamines. These figures do not take into account those amphetamines that are diverted into illegal channels or produced in black-market laboratories.

What caused such wild growth of the amphetamine market? Part of the answer may lie in the nature of the drug itself. When taken in small quantities amphetamines seem to increase alertness, decrease appetite, elevate mood, and produce a feeling of contentment. Because of these deceptive characteristics, physicians were lured into the trap. They prescribed amphetamines too liberally, unaware of the effects of long-term use.

WHAT'S IN A NAME?

There is a tendency for amphetamine abusers and pushers to tag drugs with slang names. On the surface this "jive" terminology appears to be harmless: cute, humorous, even "hip." In drug use, slang is a cover for lack of knowledge, which can be dangerous to the pill consumer. Because there is no uniformity in slang, the abuser who undoubtedly buys from illegal sources is never sure what he is swallowing. For example, "speed" may refer to methedrine or it may mean a mixture of cocaine and heroin. "Big A" is used collectively for all the amphetamines.

The table that follows provides summarized information

Some Commonly Abused Amphetamines

Chemical name	Trade name	Slang name	Medical uses
Amphet-amine	Many trade names	Ups, upses, uppers	All listed below
Amphet-amine sulfate; 6 trade names	Benzedrine, Edrisal, Nobese, Phantos	"A", bennies, pep pills, copilots	Appetite control; treatment of alcoholism, palsy
Dextroam-phetamine sulfate (17 T.N.)	Amphaplex, Dexedrine, Eskatrol, Obetrol	"A", hearts, dexies, oranges	Appetite control; mood elevator; treatment of narcolepsy, hyperactive children
Dextroam-phetamine sulfate with amphet-amine sulfate	Diphetamine	"A", pep pills, truck drivers, lid poppers	Appetite control
Metham-phetamine (16 T.N.)	Ambar, Fetamin, Methedrine, Obedrin	"A", crystals, pep pills, speed	Blood-pressure control; cerebral stimulant; treatment of barbiturate coma
D-amphet-amine Di-amphet-amine	Biphetamine	Big A	Appetite control; stimulant
Amphet-amine-like chemical; phenmet-razine	Preludin	"A"	Weight control in pregnancy

about some commonly abused amphetamines and their "pet" names of the moment. Remember that drug terminology changes frequently.

PEP PILLS WITHOUT PEP

Collectively, amphetamines are popularly known as "pep" pills. As you read this section, you will find out why this name is deceptive.

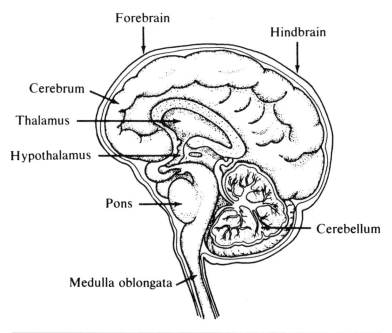

The parts of the brain have a very intimate relationship.

Like the hallucinogens, amphetamines stimulate cells of the central nervous system. However, the way amphetamines work in the brain and their effect on the body differ from the hallucinogenic drugs. As we saw in the previous chapter, the reticular formation is a region in the brain that extends through the central portion of the stem. The twofold job of the reticular formation is as follows:

1. It arouses the cerebral cortex into readiness so that the cells of the cortex can receive and interpret incoming sensory signals.
2. It regulates motor activities of the body.

Amphetamines act on the reticular system. This fact has been substantiated in research laboratories. A subject to whom amphetamine has been administered not only becomes more alert, but also renders a changed brainwave pattern on the electroencephalogram.

There is a biochemical explanation for the relationship of amphetamine to behavior. The cells of the reticular formation and the hypothalamus secrete norepinephrine. This is a neurohumor that regulates the transmission of nerve impulses by some mood-controlling nerve cells. Amphetamine increases the outpouring of norepinephrine from these nerve endings. For a reason that is not clearly understood, increased amounts of norepinephrine may act in either of two ways:

1. In hyperactive children, it has a calming effect.
2. In persons of normal or below normal activity, it stimulates them to move faster; it increases the activity of their cells.

93-18588

If amphetamine does indeed increase the vitality and activity level of people, why is the term "pep" pill misleading and dangerous? You know that increased muscular or mental activity requires cellular energy. When energy is used, it must be replaced by more energy. Chemical energy is obtained from the food that we eat and is conserved by rest. ATP molecules in our cells are banks that hold energy and dole it out as body requirements demand. When the ATP banks of energy are getting low, the nervous system gives us warning. Hunger dictates that we eat. Tiredness tells us to rest. These warning signals help us to keep a proper balance between energy intake and energy output.

Let us suppose that these warning signals are masked so that a person is not alerted to energy drain. How long can he keep going? The fact is that without energy the cells cannot work. Therefore the person collapses from total and sometimes fatal exhaustion. Herein lies one of the major dangers of amphetamine use. The pep that a person feels does not come from the pill but is drained from the energy reserves of his own cells.

Amphetamines as "reducing" pills are equally unreliable. Biochemical activity of amphetamine drugs temporarily masks sensations of hunger. Some people are helped to lose weight by these appetite suppressants. However, it is a fact that amphetamines control the appetite for only a short time. Then the pill takers usually regain their appetites and their weight. However, they continue taking pills to satisfy themselves emotionally.

The misuse of amphetamine drugs is one of the nation's most serious and most widespread drug abuse problems. There is evidence that large numbers of the adult, middle-class population are caught in the amphetamine trap. Countless lives are built around the availability of the so-called pep and diet pills. The illegal manufacture and sale of amphetamine drugs has mushroomed out of control. Amphetamines are readily available to young people. About drugs, youth has a kind of direct honesty. They openly admit taking amphetamines for "kicks." They do not hide behind the weak excuses of diet or pep.

DANGERS OF AMPHETAMINE ABUSE

Three times within the same week the same newspaper carried these headlines:

PEP PILL MAKERS
ACCUSED BY FDA

FEDERAL DRUG AGENCY
PLANS A 3-PHASE DRIVE
TO CURB MISUSE OF PEP PILLS

MOVE TO CURB THE WIDESPREAD
USE OF PEP PILLS

Why is there so much concern about amphetamine pills? The rate of abuse is growing steadily and rapidly. This means that too great a percentage of the population has become involved with pills. The consequences of amphetamine abuse are serious. Scientists now believe that abuse leads to physical addiction, homicidal behavior, brain damage, and complete mental breakdown.

Scientific study has revealed that amphetamine abuse can lead to addiction. Persons trying to withdraw from amphetamines find the experience unpleasant and painful. The person suffers extreme lethargy, fatigue, anxiety, and terrifying nightmares and may become suicidally depressed. The person is disoriented, bewildered, and confused. He is apt to be extremely irritable and demanding, driving people away just when their help is needed the most. There is a loss of self-control that may lead to violent behavior and aggressive impulses. Withdrawal from amphetamines causes headaches, difficulty in breathing, profuse sweating, and excruciating muscle cramps. The person characteristically suffers unbearably painful stomach cramps. Despite sometimes gnawing hunger, he often lacks the strength to eat.

The Food and Drug Administration is now legally restricting the use of amphetamine drugs. Drug manufacturers may produce the drugs to be used in the treatment of the following three disorders only: narcolepsy, hyperactivity in children, and extreme obesity. In the latter case a patient may be given the drug for only a short time. It is hoped that restrictive use will decrease the number of amphetamines that are produced in the legal market.

ICE, THE NEW MENACE

Methamphetamine is a synthetic stimulant that belongs to the family of the amphetamines. In its powdered form, "speed" or "crank," as it is known on the street, is taken into the body in either of two ways. It is drawn into the nostrils in a process called "snorting," or it is dissolved and injected into a vein.

Out of the underground labs in Korea, Hong Kong, and the Philippines has come a most devastating form of methamphetamine, known as "crystal meth" or "ice." Ice is a smokable drug that creates euphoria followed by severe depression.

The high from ice may last for twenty-four hours. It is followed by a terrible psychological crash that lasts for two days. Along with depression are symptoms of intense mental derangement. Persons caught in the unyielding grip of an ice crash feel that others are trying to harm them. They hallucinate and may have delusions of grandeur. Many addicts lose the ability to speak understandably and become so violent that they have to be put into restraints. Ice causes the user to be out of control.

Crystal meth overstimulates the body. An initial sign of its use is severe weight loss and the inability to sleep either night or day. The drug causes irregular heartbeat and body temperature as high as 108 degrees, which results in loss of kidney function.

The abuse of ice cuts across all social, economic, racial, and ethnic lines. However, young people in their late teens or early twenties seem to be especially drawn to it.

SUMMARY

Any drug that is capable of stimulating the central nervous system presents danger to the person if misused or abused. Amphetamines are synthetic stimulants that are useful in the treatment of certain mental disorders, but present misuse potential to the general population. Symptoms of amphetamine misuse are:

dilated pupils	excitability	muscle tremors
heavy respiration	restlessness	hallucinations
sleeplessness	talkativeness	delusions

Abuse of amphetamines has very serious consequences. Heavy users undergo mental derangement and breakdown. Symptomatic of the mental disorder is the person's belief that others are trying to persecute him or her. It is not unusual for heavy users to become violent toward others or destructive toward themselves. A recent study indicated that of amphetamine-related deaths, violence was the leading cause. Running a close second was death by stroke caused by the bursting of blood vessels in the brain. Amphetamine abuse is dangerous.

The smokable form of methamphetamine destroys users. A twenty-four-hour high is followed by a forty-eight-hour crash. Some people become so violent during the crash that they have to be put into physical restraints. Ice, the street name of crystalline methamphetamine, causes an addiction that is not easily treated.

CHAPTER 4

The Barbiturates, a Family of Sedatives

P erhaps the stress of modern living has turned us into a pill-consuming society. Self-medication with patent pills has become a way of life for many. But a large percentage of the adult population finds that "over-the-counter" pills are not efficient relievers of tension. Therefore they seek out prescribed medicines that make them feel better emotionally.

Tension takes its toll in different ways. In some people tension results in depression and loss of initiative; in others, overeating and overweight. A good number of the "depressed overeaters" seek release through amphetamines. But anxiety in a great number of people is characterized by inability to relax. These people are so "strung out" emotionally that they are always on edge. They are so

COPING WITH DRUG ABUSE

SEDATIVES, A BRIEF HISTORY

Sedatives are drugs that affect the central nervous system. Like the amphetamines, their site of action is in the medulla and the brain stem. Unlike the stimulants, sedatives have the opposite effect. They depress the involuntary activities of respiration, blood pressure, heartbeat, and cellular metabolism. Thus sedatives are called depressants.

Bromides, the first synthetic sedatives, were introduced in the 1850s. The tremendous demand for the drugs led to increased use. As you can guess, too liberal use led to abuse. Abusers of bromides (mostly adults) experienced abnormal mental conditions ranging from intoxication to complete psychological breakdown or insanity.

The bromide problem continued into the 1930s and then decreased, because by that time an impressive family of new synthetic sedatives were being marketed. The barbiturates, as they are called, are now sold under 2,500 trade names.

Actually the first barbiturate, barbital, was synthesized by two German scientists, Von Mering and Fischer, at the end of the nineteenth century. It was tested on animals and humans and seemed to have all of the desired qualities of a sedative drug. It induced sleep and reduced nervous tension. By 1912 phenobarbital, a second member of the barbiturate family, was introduced for use as a sedative. In quick succession the barbituric acid molecule became the building block for a very large family of sedatives.

MEDICAL USES OF BARBITURATES

Even today, the barbiturates are very useful medically. Because they relax the central nervous system, they are used to:

- treat conditions of high blood pressure, epilepsy, peptic ulcer, and insomnia,
- diagnose and treat mental illness,
- relax patients before and during surgery,
- induce sleep.

You may wonder why so many barbiturates are manufactured; 2,500 is an impressive number. Although these drugs are related to the core barbituric acid molecule, each drug company makes its product a little different from another in strength and in chemical composition. Thus a specific type of tablet or capsule is made to treat certain conditions. A physican prescribes the barbiturate preparation that most accurately meets the needs of the patient. For example, secobarbital (Seconal) is used to induce sleep because it relaxes the body in a short time.

RULES FOR ADMINISTERING
BARBITURATES

Note: 1 grain is equal to 64 milligrams

As a sedative	¼ grain	16 mgs
To induce sleep	1½ grains	80mgs
Before surgery	3½ grains	224 mgs
Maximum safe dosage under a doctor's supervision	9 grains	

THE PROBLEM: FROM USE TO MISUSE

The previous section discussed the legitimate uses of barbiturates, but a recent survey made by the Food and Drug
Administration indicates that:

1. One out of every four doctor's prescriptions
   ordered the use of barbiturates.
2. Over a million pounds of barbiturates per year are
   being manufactured and sold in the legal U.S.
   market.
3. Every man, woman, and child could be supplied
   with twenty-four 100-mg doses.

What does this study suggest? It indicates that there is
overuse of these drugs. Overuse can mean one thing—
abuse.

BARBITURATES, A CASE IN POINT

At twenty-two years of age, Mrs. Maria D. is a very young
housewife and mother. In age her three children are three
years, two years, and five months. Just before the last baby
was born, she and her husband moved from a city apartment into their own home in the suburbs, where they
envisioned peace, fresh air, and the leisurely pace of
"country life."

However, things did not work out as anticipated. Financial pressures forced on them a different mode of living.
Although Mr. D. still works in the city, he now has two
jobs; this means that he must leaves the house very early in
the morning and return late at night. During the week he
doesn't see the children, nor can he help with their care.

On the weekends his time is taken up with painting and other "do-it-yourself" chores.

Maria became troubled by her uncontrollable outbursts, her frequent crying jags, the constant depression. She was always wound up and ready to scream. Her stomach ached frequently and intensely. On the advice of her mother, she went to a local physician, who prescribed phenobarbital to calm her down.

For the past few weeks things have been fine; Maria takes the phenobarbs regularly. The crying of the children does not upset her as much. In fact, sometimes she is not aware of their crying and bad humor. She does not feel so lonely and strung out. Her doctor is a very nice person and quite understanding. When she told him that the medicine was losing its strength he increased the prescription dosage.

Now that you have read this case study, how would you answer the following questions:

1. What are Maria's real problems?
2. Is her doctor helping her?
3. Why did he prescribe phenobarbital?

The next section will give us some answers.

PATTERNS OF ABUSE

Barbiturates are classified by the duration of effect and the time that it takes the drug to act upon the person. Let us look at the summary information below.

The chart provides interesting information. Some barbiturates have an immediate effect on the body, and after a short time the drug's potency wears off. These are the short-acting barbiturates. The long-acting barbiturates be-

Classification of Barbiturates

Duration of effect	Generic name (trade name)	Slang term
Varying—see below	Barbiturates	Downs, downers, goof balls, barbs, sleeping pills
Long-acting* Slow-starting ———— *(6 hours or more)	Barbital-sodium mephobarbital phenobarbital	Barbs, candy, phennies
Intermediate-acting* ———— *(3–6 hours)	Amobarbital (Amytal) butabarbital butallylonal	Blues, blue heaven
Short-acting* Fast-starting ———— *(1–3 hours)	Amobarbital with secobarbital (Tunial)	Rainbows, red and blues, Christmas trees, tooies
	secobarbital (Seconal)	Reds, red devils, red birds
	Pentobarbital (Nembutal)	Yellows, yellow jackets, yellow caps

have in the opposite way. It takes longer for them to affect the body, but the sedation lasts much longer. Understandably, the short-acting barbiturates are the ones that are most commonly abused.

Medical evidence has been accumulated to show that the effects of short-acting barbiturates on the body are not unlike those of alcohol. A person can become intoxicated on barbiturates, especially the short-acting kind, which also lead to addiction. A barbiturate addict suffers from withdrawal pains and from delirium tremens, the same as an alcoholic. The behavior of barbiturate drunks varies just as it does with alcoholics. Some people become morose and withdrawn; others become talkative, argumentative, or giddy. Some people pass out from barbiturate intoxication, whereas others develop great tolerance for the drug. Most barbiturate drunks suffer from a hangover after the drug wears off.

WHO ARE THE MISUSERS AND ABUSERS?

Maria's story illustrates one type of misuser. She is a person who uses a sedative drug in order to deal with an emotional problem. To provide her with immediate relief from her symptoms of anxiety, the doctor prescribed phenobarbital. This is a long-acting, slow-starting barbiturate that is not harmful for short-term use. But if she continues to take the drug over a long period of time and in increasing amounts, she may well become an addicted abuser.

It happens that when some people develop tolerance for a barbiturate drug, they become stimulated instead of calmed by continued use. A kind of excitation and euphoria sweeps through them and gives the false feeling of increased efficiency.

Another type of abuser is illustrated by the story that follows.

For Mrs. F.G., the diet pills worked just fine. She lost fifty-five pounds, and everyone says she looks great. Since she does not wish to gain back her lost weight, Mrs. F.G. has continued taking the pills. However, in a weak moment she confessed to a friend that the pills make her irritable and keep her awake at night. Her friend recommended that she take sleeping pills. This she now does and finds that sleep without them is impossible.

DANGER SIGNALS

Dualism—a pattern of stimulation and sedation
Dualism—frequent personality changes—up to down
Dualism—habituation to a stimulant and a depressant

There are those who use barbiturates in combination with another drug. Today, the alcohol-barbiturate pattern is not uncommon. In some cases barbiturates are used to soften the effects of alcohol withdrawal. In other instances, barbiturates are taken with alcohol to heighten the effect of either drug. The alcohol-barbiturate combination is one of the leading causes of accidental death. The involuntary centers of the brain are so depressed by the action of both drugs that vital activities of heartbeat and breathing stop.

Among young people there is a very serious dimension of the barbiturate problem. Abusers of drugs such as mescaline, amphetamines, or heroin begin to inject themselves with "downers." The reasons given are varied: to soften withdrawal symptoms or to decrease hallucinations or to supplement the effects of the other drug. The case following illustrates:

Danny O. had been living in the streets for nearly two years. His "old man" threw him out of the house because he sold the family stereo, a TV set, and a few other things. "A TV a day keeps the monkey away." You see, Danny O. was a "junky" and had this daily hustle to support his habit. His "old man" should have understood that he just had to raise the "bread" to make a score. Living in the streets is quite a hassle. Sooner or later you either get busted by the cops, robbed by another junky, or gypped by some "lousy hype pusher." After experiencing all three, Danny O. decided to cut out to another city. Now this was quite a decision, because an addict cannot be far from his source of supply of "junk." But Danny O. made the move.

In his new location, he found that heroin could not be obtained so easily. The quality was poor and the price high. He therefore began "shooting" seccys (Seconal). It was not long before he had a double addiction. Fearing barbiturate withdrawal more than heroin withdrawal, Danny O. went for broke. He shot up with fifteen seccys at once. This headline appeared in the paper:

DIED OF PILLS,
NOT HEROIN
"...18, died of an overdose
of barbiturates, not heroin as
earlier thought...."

Any tranquilizer has the ability to intoxicate the user or to become habituating. The signs and symptoms of abuse closely resemble those of barbiturate drugs. The treatment is the same: difficult and prolonged.

The signs of barbiturate or tranquilizer abuse are as follows:

1. Reactions and responses are slowed.
2. Speech is thick, words are mixed up, thoughts are incoherent.
3. Behavior is unpredictable; one minute a person may be calm, next minute upset and enraged.
4. Vision is distorted.
5. Effect of the same drug is variable on the same

person, leading to confusion and accidental overdose.
6. Person appears as if in an alcoholic oblivion.
7. Person lacks the pep or the desire to do anything.
8. Barbiturate abuse leads to addiction.
9. Overdose leads to death.

BARBITURATES SIGNAL DANGER

Barbiturates are physically addictive. This means that a tissue tolerance develops in which the abuser must take necessary doses of the drug in order to get the desired effect. To avoid withdrawal pains the person must continue "popping" large doses of pills.

Barbiturate withdrawal is difficult, costly, and dangerous. If the drug is suddenly withheld from an addict, the addicted person suffers withdrawal sickness. This is an agony of cramps, vomiting, and delirium. If uncontrolled, convulsions and death follow.

A barbiturate addict must be cured slowly. Under the close supervision of a doctor, he or she is given the drug in decreasing amounts until the body can do without it. The treatment is time-consuming and costly. Very few barbiturate addicts are cured.

A WORD ABOUT TRANQUILIZERS

In recent years a number of synthetic sedatives and tranquilizers have flooded the drug market. You may recognize some of these names:

Miltown	Valium	Placidal
Equalin	Noludar	Doriden
Librium	Valmid	Somnos

Any tranquilizer has the ability to intoxicate the user or to become habituating. The signs and symptoms of abuse closely resemble those of barbiturate drugs. The treatment is the same: difficult and prolonged.

Studies conducted in the Netherlands and reported in the July, 1982, *Journal of Science* show that a single 10-milligram dose of Valium seriously impairs the navigational abilities of expert automobile drivers. The reaction time of expert drivers was measured in experiments designed to determine what effect, if any, Valium has on driving ability. The experimental subjects were divided into three groups. One group was given the 10-milligram dose of Valium. A second group was given a placebo; a third group, nothing. Each group consisted of ten subjects. The drivers in the control groups (placebo and no tranquilizer) drove normally and safely. Three of the experimental subjects crossed lanes into what would have been oncoming traffic. Five of the experimental group drove in a wavering fashion, frequently crossing lanes without warning. All ten drivers in the experimental group were affected by the drug, some more than others.

QUAALUDES: THE BARBITURATE MIMIC

Sold under the trade names of Quaalude, Parest, Sopor, Optimil, and Somnafac, methyl qualone is a dangerous hypnotic sedative. In one year, the grim statistics caused by this drug were 313 deaths from withdrawal or overdose and 53 suicides. Human destruction brought about by Quaalude is so frightening that all methaqualone derivatives have been placed on the dangerous-drug list. Possession of the drug with intent to sell is a felony.

Methaqualone mimics the barbiturates in giving the abuser a temporary sense of security; it then plunges the person into a dark depression. Abusers tend to lose interest in everything except popping these pills. Many people experience visual hallucinations leading to such acute anxiety that suicidal attempts are not uncommon. Like the barbiturates, methaqualone builds tissue tolerance and thus addiction. Withdrawal is dangerous. If withdrawal is not carried out under the constant care of a doctor, the addict in all probability will suffer from hemorrhaging of the stomach lining, depression of the respiratory center, convulsions, and death.

SUMMARY

Barbiturate abuse has been a problem of many middle- and upper-class adults for the past thirty-five years. Many of these abusers became medically addicted before doctors realized the tissue tolerance potential of the barbiturate drugs and their derivatives.

Today we are faced with a grimmer picture of barbiturate abuse, because now these drugs obtained through illegal channels have been placed in the hands of teenagers and very young adults. The pattern of abuse varies. It may be of the "pill head" type in which the person takes multiple barbiturates for the intoxication effects, or downers may be taken as a supplement to another drug.

The pattern of abuse really doesn't matter; the end effect is the same: addiction. Less than 5 percent of those addicted to barbiturates or Quaaludes ever successfully kick the habit.

CHAPTER ◇ 5

Heroin, the
Hard Narcotic

A narcotic is a drug that produces sleep or stupor and at the same time relieves pain. Because narcotic drugs have the ability to make people insensible to pain, they are known medically as analgesic drugs and popularly as painkillers. The greatest natural source of analgesics is opium.

Opium comes from the poppy, *Papayer somniferum*, which thrives in the hot, dry climates of Turkey, China, India, Iran, and Mexico. After the delicate red, white, or purple flowers bloom, laborers make a longitudinal slit in the unripe seed pods. From this wound oozes a rubbery sap, which is collected, pressed into bricks, and dried. Thus opium is harvested and prepared for export. In legal laboratories of pharmaceutical houses in Europe and the United States, raw opium is processed into medicinal products. Actually, opium is a complex substance that consists of nearly twenty alkaloids. These are nitrogen compounds that have physiological effects on man and animals. Some

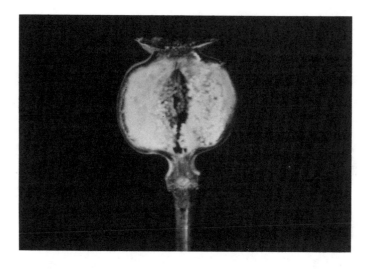

COURTESY CAROLINA BIOLOGICAL SUPPLY HOUSE
Opium poppy seed capsule

of the better-known opium alkaloids are morphine, co-
deine, laudanum, and metapon.

THE HISTORICAL USES OF THE OPIATES

The use of opium to relieve pain, to diminish anxiety, and
to produce a feeling of dreamy well-being has been known
to man for centuries. Probably as early as 4000 B.C. the
opium poppy was cultivated by the Sumerians as a source
of opium. It is believed that from Sumer knowledge of
opium spread through Egypt, Asia Minor, Greece, and
Rome. Two thousand years ago the Roman Emperor
Tiberius moved his entire court to the isle of Capri so that
he could be near the opium poppy.

The seventeenth-century English pioneer of medicine
Thomas Sydenham wrote these words:

"Among the remedies which it has pleased almighty God to give to man to relieve his sufferings none is so efficacious as opium."

Neither Dr. Sydenham nor scores of medical practitioners who followed him knew about the harmful effects of opium and its products. In England during the eighteenth century laudanum, a preparation of opium dissolved in alcohol, was sold on the open market in unlimited amounts. Doctors of the day prescribed laudanum to deaden the pain of toothache. Little thought was given to the fact that it was addicting. However, Samuel Taylor Coleridge, a nineteenth-century writer, described his addiction to laudanum as "the accursed habit," "this wretched vice, a species of madness...a derangement, an utter impotence of the volition." He blamed his addiction for his neglect of his family.

A pair of seemingly unrelated circumstances popularized another opium product. The first of these events took place in 1805, when a German pharmacist's assistant, Wilhelm Frederic Serturner, isolated morphine from opium. Named after Morpheus, the Greek god of dreams, morphine has very remarkable analgesic properties. The second event took place about thirty years later: the hypodermic needle was invented by a Scotsman, Dr. Alexander Wood. These two happenings began the practice of introducing analgesics into the bloodstream by injection. By the middle 1800s doctors were prescribing morphine to patients for relief of pain from neuralgia. The unlimited use of morphine in Europe and the United States, especially during the Civil War, brought about widespread problems of morphine addiction.

In 1898 it was thought that the solution to the morphine problem was found. At this time German scientists pro-

COURTESY CAROLINA BIOLOGICAL SUPPLY COMPANY

Ripened pod of an opium poppy.

COURTESY CAROLINA BIOLOGICAL SUPPLY COMPANY

Opium seed pod that has been slit. Note how gummy opium oozes from the slits.

duced diacetylmorphine by chemically altering the morphine molecule. The new product was initially hailed as the perfect analgesic, the nonaddicting pain reliever. However, it was soon discovered that this by-product of morphine is even more addicting than the parent molecule. In fact, use of the drug was quickly terminated. It was then that it slipped into the hands of the underworld. We know this drug today by the name heroin.

MEDICINAL USES OF THE OPIATES

In recent years the medical use of opium and its products has decreased. Synthetic analgesics have been developed that are not as addicting as the opiates. However, use is still made of certain opium preparations.

The table below summarizes current use of opium derivatives.

Name of Drug	Use	Precautions
Opium Mixtures Donnagel Pantopon Parepectplin Paregoric	To relieve spasms of the intestinal tract. Decreased pain.	ALL PREPARATIONS LISTED IN THIS TABLE ARE CAPABLE OF ADDICTING THE USER
Opium Derivatives Codeine Morphine Bentley's compound	 Cough suppressant Analgesic drug; to relieve severe pain. To induce sleep in wild animals. Not administered to humans.	
Synthetic analgesics (based on morphine molecule) Demerol Benzomorphans Methadone	 Analgesic Analgesic To treat heroin addicts	

DANGEROUS ASPECTS OF THE OPIATES

All of the drugs that are obtained from opium have two serious defects that present danger to users. First, opiate drugs depress respiration. This means that the rate at which the person obtains and uses oxygen is slowed. It is possible for respiration to be so depressed so that it stops. Of course, the person dies. When an addict dies of drug overdose, it means that his respiration rate was fatally depressed.

The opiate drugs are known as hard narcotics because of their other defect: they are highly addictive.

An addicted person:

Dependency	Is mentally and physically incapable of thinking or accomplishing without the drug.
Tissue tolerance	Must take increasingly larger doses of the drug of get a satisfying effect.
Withdrawal	Becomes painfully ill with muscle cramps and vomiting when his drug-taking is interrupted.

HEROIN, THE ILLEGAL STEPCHILD

Heroin is an opiate drug. It is obtained by a chemical process during which the stems in morphine molecules are rearranged. Unlike its parent molecule, heroin has no medical use at all. Its pain-killing ability is inferior, and its addicting potential is high. The manufacture and sale of heroin is illegal, yet this drug continues to pour into the United States from the illegal laboratories of France and Mexico at an alarming rate.

Heroin addiction among young people has become a serious national problem. At one time the use of "horse" seemed to be localized in pockets of poor areas in the large cities. Now this is no longer true. The "mighty horse" has galloped from the urban ghettos into the affluent suburbs and into smaller cities. It has transcended all barriers of social class, race, and economic level. It is now the most outstanding and vicious abuser of the young.

Money is the motive for dealers in death and destruction. For $1,000 an investor can buy enough heroin in France to sell wholesale for $1 million in the U.S. Retailers will get a minimum of $50 million from that single $1,000 purchase.

THE EFFECTS OF HEROIN ON THE BODY

Heroin may be taken into the body in one of four ways. An addict may draw up the heroin powder through the nasal passages; this is known as "snorting." Heroin may be injected into a vein; this is known as "mainlining." Some addicts inject the dissolved drug under the skin in a process called "skin-popping." Heroin that is 45 percent pure becomes smokable. Addicts put the drug into a pipe, ignite it, and draw the heroin vapor into their lungs. No matter how heroin is taken into the body, it travels through the bloodstream and invades every body cell.

By some mechanism not fully understood, heroin becomes involved in the biochemical metabolism of cells. It affects the cells in the medulla of the brain, slowing their activity, which results in depressed respiration and slower heartbeat. In addition, the effect on the medulla causes abnormal reflex behavior. For example, the pupils of the addict's eyes dilate and contract in response to the level of heroin in the blood, not to light. This is why the wearing of dark glasses even at night is a hallmark of heroin addiction.

Repeated use of heroin causes some type of adaptation in body cells that prevents their working well without the drug. It seems that heroin may be involved with calcium metabolism. When heroin is denied to an addict, there is a reduction in the calcium stores in the blood and in the involuntary muscle tissue. This leads to cramps (muscle tetany) and pain. The rotting teeth and bone breaks of heroin addicts may be related to faulty use of calcium caused by the drug.

EFFECTS OF HEROIN ADDICTION

There is no pleasant side of addiction. The life of a junky is ugly—disgusting, demeaning, downhill all the way. Following is a summary of some of the physical and mental effects of addiction:

Needle tracks along the inner arms and outer legs are telltale marks of mainlining. Frequently ulcerated, festering sores develop as a result of using dirty needles.

Malnutrition goes hand in hand with addiction. Food has no taste appeal to a junky. He is interested only in drugs. He loses a great deal of weight and becomes highly susceptible to all kinds of disease.

Nodding and drowsiness are distinguishing characteristics of heroin addicts. Shortly after a "fix" they fall asleep. Even when walking, they can drop off into drug-induced sleep. Thus it is not unusual for addicts to have serious accidents or falls or to burn themselves up because they have no control over themselves.

Diseases of the blood follow addicts as fleas follow dogs. Along with the dirty needles that they share come blood

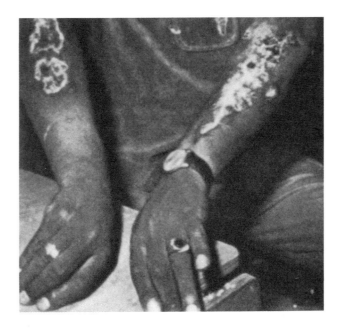

COURTESY BUREAU OF NARCOTICS AND DANGEROUS
DRUGS. U.S. DEPARTMENT OF JUSTICE

Ulcerated arms of a heroin mainliner.

poisoning, hepatitis, jaundice, syphilis, malaria, and bacterial endocarditis, and AIDS.

Personal neglect and poor hygiene are directly related to heroin addiction. Junkies lose the ability to care about themselves and ignore all the rules of cleanliness. They do not bathe, change their clothes, brush their teeth, or sleep in clean places. It is not uncommon for addicts to have body lice.

Abnormal personality and unpleasant behavior patterns and habits make an addict unbearable. His entire life's drive is subverted to getting drugs. No one can love this animal-person who lies, cheats, steals, and may even kill for a nickel (five-dollar) bag of junk.

THE METHADONE MAINTENANCE TREATMENT PROGRAM

Methadone is a man-made analgesic drug that has a structure similar to the morphine molecule. In 1963 Dr. Vincent Dole, a metabolic researcher, and Dr. Marie Nyswander, a psychiatrist, began an experimental program designed to withdraw addicts from heroin. They found that by building tolerance to methadone they could decrease or block an addict's appetite for heroin. Based on the work of these investigators, the methadone maintenance treatment program gained wide acceptance in New York State as a means of treating drug addicts.

The program offers treatment to addicts who are eighteen years of age and older. The addict must meet certain specifications before he is admitted for treatment. First, he must be addicted to heroin only. Persons with double addictions are not accepted. Second, the addict must not have difficult psychiatric problems. The purpose of the program is to withdraw as many addicts as possible and return them to society as functioning useful individuals.

At first the methadone maintenance treatment program functioned very simply. After a thorough physical examination in a hospital, the tolerance of an addict was determined. He was assigned to one of the many outpatient clinics in New York City, to which he reported daily. Each day he was given methadone orally, usually in orange juice. The patient then left a urine sample, which was checked for heroin. Even if an addict does use heroin after taking methadone, the heroin has no effect.

ABUSE OF THE METHADONE MAINTENANCE TREATMENT PROGRAM

Methadone maintenance functioned well when it served a small number of heroin addicts. Care such as this is costly. To involve more addicts, many methadone clinics were established throughout metropolitan New York. However, the quality of care degenerated. Gone are the physical and psychiatric cores of the program. Addicts on register at the various clinics are merely handed daily doses of methadone with little or no supervision. As could be expected, strange things occur.

Addicts are unreliable and not trustworthy. Many sell their methadone supply and use the money to buy heroin. Others use methadone in combination with other drugs to achieve the desired high. There are those who have never been addicted to heroin but who became methadone addicts because the drug was readily available.

There is no doubt that the initial arguments against methadone treatment for heroin addicts have some merit. It is certainly true that methadone is itself addicting and that its use is just substituting one addiction for another. Continuing dependence rather than true rehabilitation does not restore an addict to a useful life. Without psychiatric therapy and close supervision, the methadone user remains an addict.

THE HEROIN MIMIC

Talwin, a morphine-like synthetic analgesic, has become the newest phenomenon in drug abuse. Talwin, a painkiller, produces a euphoric effect not unlike that of heroin. Many abusers mix talwin with the antihistamine pyribenzamine. When combined, the two create what is called the

"T's and blues." Legislation has been enacted to place restrictions on the sale of this drug.

SUMMARY

Getting involved with hard narcotics is not a game. It is not even a fair gamble, because the user is always the loser. Opiate drugs are known as hard narcotics because they build tissue tolerance, which leads to addiction. Heroin, the most abused opiate, invades every cell in the body. As a result, the user cannot function in the everyday routines of living. He becomes a heroin slave, a junky. Synthetic drugs are just as dangerous and often more difficult to withdraw from.

Don't be fooled. Whether it is called "H," junk, Harry, horse, smack, white stuff, or joy powder, heroin is a bad scene.

CHAPTER ◇ 6

Cocaine, the Fantasy Maker

In one way or another all people leave this world temporarily. Some people are transported into the world of make-believe by daydreaming; others through sleep. Some escape by reading; others watch movies. There are those who use drugs as a temporary escape, only to find that the addiction that follows is very permanent. The user becomes trapped in a misshapen world of fantasy from which there is no escape.

THE SOURCE

Erythroxylon coca, the coca tree, grows high in the Andes Mountains of South America. Certain Indians of Peru and Bolivia chew coca leaves to obtain the mild stimulation that helps them fight fatigue caused by the high altitudes at which they work. Leaf-chewing seems not to harm the user because the stimulating chemical extracted is in such small quantities. When they come down from the high altitudes of the Andes, the Indians stop chewing coca leaves, for there is no longer any need. However, the work of these coca farmers is to pick and process the leaves into a paste from which the drug cocaine is extracted.

The coca leaf contains many active alkaloids, of which cocaine is only one. Mid-nineteenth-century German scientists introduced pure cocaine for use as a medicinal drug. In 1855 a chemist named Gardeken isolated cocaine from the coca leaf. It was given the name cocaine by a research physician named Niemann in 1859. In 1883, Dr. Theodor Aschenbrandt, a German army physician, tried out the new drug on a group of Bavarian soldiers. He reported that it had very positive effects and cited the soldiers' increased ability to overcome fatigue.

Shortly after Dr. Aschenbrandt's published report, Dr.

COURTESY BUREAU OF NARCOTICS AND DANGEROUS DRUGS. U.S. DEPARTMENT OF JUSTICE

Coca leaves and various forms of cocaine.

Sigmund Freud, an Austrian neurologist, began using the drug to treat his own depression and chronic fatigue. He also tested the drug on two of his patients. Both he and his patients received favorable initial results from the use of cocaine, a circumstance that resulted in Freud's extending its use to cure a personal friend of morphine addiction. Sadly, the morphine addict under treatment could not control his use of cocaine and kept increasing the dosage until he was using very great amounts of the drug. The results were frightening. Von Fleischl-Marxow, the morphine addict turned cocaine addict, developed severe mental disturbances. He developed a psychosis described as paranoia, exhibiting a mental state known as formication. This is a type of hallucination in which the afflicted believes insects or snakes are crawling under the skin. Formication is brought about also by methamphetamine. Because of the serious symptoms that cocaine caused in his friend, Freud stopped using the drug personally and on patients.

Around the turn of the century, cocaine use spread to the United States, where it was imbibed as a popular tonic. Many myths developed about its use, including the erroneous belief that cocaine was more readily abused by the lower socioeconomic classes. Actually, its greatest use was among the more privileged classes. The Harrison Narcotic Act of 1914 classified cocaine as a narcotic, subject to the same penalties as opium and its derivatives.

COCAINE, THE SUPER STIMULANT

Cocaine is an odorless, sometimes crystalline, sometimes fluffy white, powder. So potent is the pure cocaine hydrochloride that a one-gram dose taken into the body is lethal. Because very small quantities of "coke" induce euphoria, drug dealers "cut" the pure powder with such adulterants as mannite, dextrose, lactose, tartaric acid, or sodium bicarbonate.

At one time cocaine was used widely as a local anesthetic. The newer synthetic drugs Procaine and Novocain are now used in its place. Although cocaine is classified as a narcotic under the federal narcotic laws, it does not have the properties of the opiate drugs. It bears no resemblance to heroin or morphine in either chemical composition or physiological activity. Actually cocaine is a stimulant, resembling both the amphetamines and the hallucinogens in activity. As you may recall from previous chapters, the stimulants and the hallucinogens are capable of inducing euphoria along with hallucinations. This is just what cocaine does in large doses.

Cocaine is taken into the bloodstream by either of two methods: snorting or mainlining. When drawn through the nose, the drug is absorbed slowly through the mucous membranes of the nose. Snorting cocaine delays its effects for a few minutes, but a heightened level of intensity is experienced by the user for thirty minutes. When cocaine is injected into the bloodstream, its effects are felt immediately but last for only ten minutes.

Because it is a powerful stimulant, cocaine immediately works on the central nervous system. It raises the pulse and respiration rates, increases the body temperature, and elevates the blood pressure. It constricts the blood vessels and dilates the pupils of the eyes. Cocaine induces a kind of hyperexcitement in the user, bringing about a euphoria that seems to stimulate sexual desire. Soon after the drug reaches the bloodstream, the user gets an instant rush to the head, a "high" that lasts for about half an hour. During the rush, the user is prompted toward activity and experiences a state of reduced fatigue and appetite. Users claim that cocaine induces the ability to think more clearly and increases their muscular strength. Researchers tell us that these attributes are simply imagined.

Researchers have found that there is a wide variety of reactions to cocaine. Even small doses of high-grade cocaine induce a diversity of feelings among users. Some stress a feeling of happiness and well-being. Other users say that they feel more energetic and still others that it increases their ability to approach and solve difficult problems. Whatever the induced feelings, they are temporary and very short-lived. Some people feel depressed after the effects of the drug wear off.

COCAINE, THE TROUBLEMAKER

It was the first time for Len Bias. This talented University of Maryland basketball star had never used drugs. In celebration of his having been drafted by the Boston Celtics (a professional basketball team), Bias allowed "friends" to entice him to snort cocaine. He died from cocaine intoxication. The cocaine interrupted the normal electrical control of his heartbeat, resulting in heart seizure and cardiac arrest (stopping of heartbeat).

The medical examiner found that the cocaine in Len Bias's blood measured 6.5 milligrams per liter. A milligram is a thousandth part of a gram; a gram is the size of a small green pea. A liter is a fluid measure having the approximate volume of a quart. So you see that it takes very little cocaine to cause trouble. This small amount of a drug ended the life and promising career of a young athlete.

COCAINE DAMAGES THE BODY

Cocaine has severe physical effects on the body, particularly the blood vessels and the nervous system. Cocaine causes narrowing of the blood vessels, which in turn brings about a quick rise in blood pressure and a quickening of the heart rate. As in the case of Len Bias, it can also trigger fatal heart rhythms. Any effect on the blood vessels can increase the heart's need for more oxygen-rich blood to nourish its cells. If the oxygen shortage is mild and brief, the person may suffer only chest pains (angina). However, if the shortage is sustained, heart cells die and the person suffers a heart attack. Cocaine assaults the body in a number of ways. It narrows the blood vessels that lead away from the heart to the brain. These blood vessels are the arteries. Narrowing of the arteries to the brain causes stroke, seizures, tremors, delirium, and psychosis. An increasing number of young people are suffering from these cocaine-induced disorders. Fatal seizures can result from just one dose of cocaine.

Cocaine hurts the body in other ways. It destroys cells in the liver, interfering with important functions of this vital gland that breaks down substances, readying them for excretion from the body. Cocaine causes the lungs to fill with fluid, resulting in loss of breathing capacity. It damages the cells in the lining of the nose, causing nosebleeds and loss of the sense of smell. It damages the reproductive system. Men who use cocaine for a long time become impotent.

COCAINE DAMAGES BABIES

Pregnant women who use cocaine endanger the lives of their babies before they are born and after birth. The use of cocaine during pregnancy can decrease the oxygen supply to the fetus, which can either kill the fetus or induce premature delivery. In many cases lack of oxygen in the blood supply to the uterus causes separation of the placenta from the uterine wall. Loss of the placenta causes spontaneous abortion of the fetus.

Cocaine-exposed babies usually are abnormally small at birth and have smaller than normal head and brain. In many cases the genital and urinary organs including the kidneys are malformed, resulting in life-threatening infections. An unusual number of crib deaths occur among cocaine-exposed babies.

Babies with cocaine in their system are in danger of a host of abnormalities. A stroke that cuts off the blood supply to the small intestine causes it to shrink and become useless; a baby so afflicted cannot digest food. Cocaine can damage the brain and nervous system of a child, preventing him or her from learning and from behaving acceptably. Learning disabilities and uncontrolled behavior lead to failure in school and in society.

COCAINE AFFECTS THE MIND

The symptoms of chronic cocaine abuse are serious. The drug has the ability to unmask psychopathic tendencies. It induces delusions of persecution and grandeur, jealousy and violence, insomnia and muscular unrest. Frequently, cocaine habitués experience nervous excitability, over-sensitivity to noise, mood swings, memory loss and disturbances, compulsive scribbling known as graphomania, and anxiety. They may suffer from auditory and visual hallucinations that give credence to the belief that someone is persecuting or oppressing them. A chronic cocaine user is a dangerous person who is capable of committing brutal crimes. Minor frustrations may cause suicide or homicide attempts. In addition to mental disturbances, cocaine abuse causes physiological disorders: feebleness, emaciation, digestive disorders, nausea, vomiting, loss of appetite, fast pulse, impotence. In the late stages of chronic cocaine abuse, paralysis and convulsions may occur.

SIGNS AND SYMPTOMS OF ABUSE

A cocaine abuser appears energetic and euphoric. But the person feels "high" for a relatively short time and is then left depressed and full of anxiety. When under the influence of the drug, the pupils of the user's eyes are dilated and fixed. Tremors may occur.

Some cocaine users seek sedation with other drugs. The cocaine "high" often gives the user more excitement than he can bear. At one time cocaine abusers mixed the drug with heroin, producing a product known as a "speedball." Double trouble resulted from this practice; the person not only increased the need for cocaine, but also developed a tissue tolerance for heroin.

Chronic cocaine use has serious effects on the body and the mind. As its use has become more widespread, physicians have been able to assess more accurately its harm to the user. Because the natural pleasure centers of cocaine users' brains become changed, they never feel pleasure without the drug. In fact, cocaine upsets the normal balance of chemicals necessary to move nerve impulses from one nerve cell to another. These chemicals, *neurotransmitters*, are released by the ends of nerve cells to stimulate the adjoining group of nerve cells. Some of the neurotransmitters are then reabsorbed into certain nerve cells for recycling. Cocaine prevents the reabsorption of three neurotransmitters. One of them helps people to be energetic, assertive, and alert; a second regulates sleep; and a third produces sensations of pleasure and well-being. Because the chemical balance of the nervous system has been disrupted by cocaine, the chronic user becomes dependent upon the drug to feel good. Certain symptoms control the lives of chronic abusers: depression, belief that someone or something will harm them (paranoia), hallucinations, difficulty in sleeping, loss of appetite, and inability to experience pleasure.

At one time it was believed that cocaine was not addictive. It is now known, however, that chronic users experience withdrawal sickness when denied the drug. The withdrawal syndrome (a series of symptoms) lasts about fourteen days. The symptoms include depression, extreme fatigue, irrational fear, nervousness, excessive perspiration, chills, nausea, vomiting, sensation of bugs crawling under the skin, and an unrelenting craving for cocaine.

Treatment for cocaine addiction is costly and time-consuming. Cocaine has to be removed from the addict's system completely. Then he or she must receive individual and group therapy to modify the behavior. Some addicts require treatment with antidepressant medication as they receive intense psychotherapy. Once addicted, a person is never really free of cocaine. Rehabilitation becomes a lifelong process.

SUMMARY

Cocaine is no longer the expensive drug that it once was. It is readily available on the streets, sold by people who care nothing for human life. It is adulterated with anything that will keep the dealers' profits high. There is no quality control for the buyer.

Nor is cocaine the harmless drug it was once thought to be. It causes the user severe physical and psychological problems. Cocaine can become addicting. In popular language cocaine is called:

coke	snowbirds
snow	Cecil
happy dust	stardust
"C"	Bernice
gold dust	white girl
flake	speedball

All of these mean cocaine, the fantasy maker, cocaine, the troublemaker. Cocaine is classified as a narcotic drug, making its sale and possession illegal. A person found in possession of cocaine faces stiff penalties.

CHAPTER 7

Crack, The National Nightmare

People become involved with cocaine to feel better. However, to continue to "feel better" they must take more cocaine. After the coke high wears off, they begin to feel depressed, anxious, irritable, or even suicidal. The truth of the matter is that cocaine destroys the pleasure centers in the brain, and the user must look for a stronger substance that will provide a better high. Underground chemists have helped by devising chemical means to change cocaine. This chapter tells the story: from freebase to crack.

FREEBASE: THE OTHER COCAINE

We have discussed ways in which cocaine is taken into the body by snorting and mainlining. In addition, a special chemical process enables cocaine to be smoked.

The white crystalline powder known as cocaine is really the chemical compound cocaine hydrochloride, a combination of cocaine alkaloid and hydrochloric acid. The presence of hydrochloric acid prevents the compound from vaporizing when heated.

To alter cocaine so that it can be smoked, it is treated with a solution of baking soda and the solvent petroleum ether. When these substances are mixed together, a layer of liquid containing cocaine forms on top. This layer is removed into a separate dish and allowed to evaporate. The cocaine produced by this process is known as *freebase*. It is put into a water pipe and heated with a propane torch to turn the cocaine into smoke. Smoking cocaine processed in this way is known as *freebasing*. It is common knowledge that comedian Richard Pryor was badly burned from an explosion of ether as he was preparing freebase.

Smoking freebase gives the user an instantaneous high that lasts for only a few minutes. Users like the intensity of the "rush," and some freebase several times a day. However, the process is dangerous because petroleum ether is highly flammable and explosive. Therefore, unscrupulous chemists in the drug trade have devised a simpler method of changing cocaine into a smokable form; the resulting drug is now sold on the market under the name of *crack*.

"I dropped out of high school at seventeen and went to work in a restaurant. I was making $130 a week and spending $100 a week on drugs. Then I began freebasing. From freebasing I moved on to crack, which I began doing all the time.

"My behavior changed. I got really selfish—thinking only about myself and crack. My mother realized I was on drugs and tried to get me to stop or get help. But I didn't want help. I just wanted to get high.

"My life sank to the pits. I stopped working and started stealing money from my mother's pocketbook

- A parking meter coin collector disappeared with $4,000 in quarters. He later turned himself in to the police, informing them of his addiction to crack.

These and many stories like them appear in daily newspapers telling of the criminal acts of crack addicts. In the next section we shall see how crack pushes those under its influence into acts of violence and irresponsibility.

CRACK AND THE BODY "HOT SPOTS"

Crack is taken into the body by smoking. The crystalline chips are put into a glass pipe and smoked or crushed and smoked in a marijuana joint. When heated the chips crackle—thus the name crack.

Heating crack changes it to smoke, which is inhaled, drawn into the lungs, and then diffused rapidly into the bloodstream. Circulating blood transports the dissolved cocaine to the brain, where it has immediate effect. Snorted cocaine reaches the brain in two or three minutes, but smoked cocaine reaches the brain in seconds. The immediate effect of smoking is called a "rush," a sudden high caused by the assault on the brain and central nervous system of almost pure cocaine. The central nervous system responds by stimulating certain body reactions: increased body temperature, involuntary movement of muscles, and overstimulation of the pleasure centers in the brain. The high lasts for a short period of time, ranging from ten minutes to half an hour. Crack is used up very quickly.

When the high level of chemical activity in the brain cells stops, a condition called a *rebound* is produced. The rebound or "crash" is characterized by severe depression. The person feels powerless, lacks self-confidence, becomes lethargic (loses energy), and develops negative feelings about self.

Even in a short period of time, regular use of crack produces abnormal effects in the brain. The brain's pleasure centers slow down, responding slowly. As the pleasure centers lose their ability to respond, crack users increase their dose in an effort to regain the rush, the high from which they originally obtained pleasure. The attempt to get pleasure from the drug becomes so compelling that many addicts devote their entire being to obtaining and smoking crack.

Crack pervades the body, touching and destroying its organs. The tissues and organs affected by crack are called *hot spots*. Remember that crack is pure cocaine that has been chemically changed to be vaporized so that it can be inhaled. When cocaine smoke (vapor) reaches the blood, it is dissolved in the plasma. Circulating blood transports the dissolved cocaine first to the brain, where the pleasure centers are stimulated; the rest is deposited in other body organs.

Crack and the Skin. The skin covering the face is affected. Crack abnormally stimulates the oil glands, causing them to oversecrete. The skin becomes oily. The pores clog, causing pimples and acne. In some way crack interferes with skin coloring, giving it a yellowish or grayish cast. The change in color probably indicates liver damage and is a signal of jaundice caused by damaged blood cells.

Crack and the Blood Vessels. Crack increases the blood pressure markedly. This means that blood is racing through the arteries and arterioles at a rate that can only harm the body. In areas where crack is a major problem, doctors are reporting an "epidemic" of fatal brain hemorrhages among addicts.

The blood is contained in vessels and does not touch tissue cells. When a blood vessel that serves the brain bursts, hemorrhage occurs. Blood leaks onto delicate tissues, clots, and destroys brain cells.

In a letter to the *Journal* of the American Medical Association, a group of physicians from an inner-city hospital reported that seven crack users—men aged 21 to 40 years—suffered hemorrhages within a three-month period. Six died; one was left in a coma. It is unusual for brain hemorrhage to occur in young people in their 20's and for so many to occur within three months in the same locality. Dr. Alan Tuchman, head of the neurology department at Lincoln Hospital in New York, said, "We think it [brain hemorrhage] might be related to crack, since this drug has become very common now."

Crack and the Eyes. When people wear dark glasses at night, it is usually not a matter of style, but a signal of drug abuse. Cocaine dissolved in the blood affects the muscles that open and close the pupils in the eyes. Under normal circumstances, pupils close automatically in response to bright light and open to admit light when its intensity is low.

Crack causes the pupillary muscles to dilate and remain open, becoming unable to respond to brightness or dimness of light. The eyes then become sensitive to light. Users often see halos, also called "snowlights," surrounding objects on which they attempt to focus. They see indistinctly. To improve their vision and reduce sensitivity to light, crack addicts wear dark glasses all the time.

Crack and the Heart. The heart is made of strong cardiac muscle that beats without your control. The heartbeat is inborn and automatic and, in part, is monitored by the autonomic nervous system. Crack changes the normal rhythm of the heartbeat, speeding it up to 30 to 50 percent above its normal rate. Crack also interferes with the regularity of the heartbeat, making it skip beats and then double up on contractions. Physicians expect that fatal heart attacks will become commonplace among teenagers and young adults as the crack epidemic spreads.

Crack and the Lungs. You know that your lungs have the vital function of admitting oxygen to the blood. Your lungs also remove the waste gas carbon dioxide from the circulating blood. Chemicals that damage lung tissue destroy the air sacs and thus prevent the proper exchange of gases between the internal body organs and the outside environment.

Crack affects the tubes that lead into the lungs. The tubes are the *bronchi* (bronchus, s.) and their smaller branches called *bronchioles*. Crack prevents the bronchioles from working properly; they fill up with mucus and become inflamed. Ultimately, crack users develop bronchitis, evidenced by their constant coughing and hoarseness of voice.

Crack and the Body Muscles. Body movements are controlled by two sets of muscles. The involuntary or smooth muscles oversee the movements that you cannot control at will. The movement of the intestines, pupillary reflex, and the work of the kidneys are some of the muscular activities that you cannot control. But you can walk about, ride a bike, swim, and hop because of your voluntary or striated muscles.

Muscles move in an organized fashion because of the action of sliding elements that make up the microscopic muscle bundles. Crack affects the chemical substances that make the muscles work. It overstimulates them as it does everything else in the body and causes the muscle fibers to contract without need. It is not unusual for crack users to display facial tics or involuntary jerks of the body caused by faulty signals to the muscle fibers. Crack has been known to cause convulsions.

Crack and Body Weight.   Severe weight loss accompanies continuous crack use. Crack overstimulates the pleasure centers in the brain but depresses those brain areas that signal body needs. A person on crack literally forgets to eat and drink because his or her appetite control centers are not working. When the body's nutritional needs are not satisfied, malnutrition and its accompanying health defects set in.

Crack and the Emotions.   Emotions are feelings. Emotions are the psychological measures of mood and character. Every human being experiences changes in mood. Sometimes we are happy and at other times a bit depressed. But the changes vary within a "normal" range.

The emotions of crack users are always in extremes: excessively high and euphoric or devastatingly low. When high on crack, a user is overwhelmed by a false sense of power and might. He feels strengths and abilities that he really does not have and gives off a deceptive aura of self-confidence. These feelings of strength and self-confidence last only as long as the high; the mood of well-being disappears, and the person crashes into a bottomless pit of depression.

Other unpleasant emotions accompany the depression. The person becomes irritable and suspicious. The combination of these emotions results in paranoia, fear and suspicion of others. Law enforcement agents inform us that crack users are capable of great violence driven by the paranoia induced by the drug. They constantly look behind them as they walk down the street, fearful of being followed by someone who will do them harm. Irritability, short temper, and fear are the emotions that drive them into committing destructive acts.

Crack and Behavior.   Strictly speaking, behavior means everything that a person does in response to changes in his or her environment. Both the internal environment of the body and the external environment govern behavioral responses. The external environment of the crack user is confined to those aspects of existence where s/he can obtain the crack necessary to satisfy an insatiable habit. The internal environment of the body is certainly changed by frequent assault of almost pure cocaine on the fluids and tissues that compose the body organs. Thus, crack users exhibit abnormal behavior patterns.

> "I've been getting high since I was ten, and I dropped out of school in the seventh grade when I was thirteen. My mother worked, and all I did was hang out with my friends and get high. I started stealing from my mother's pocketbook. I would take the support checks that my father sent and forge her name and cash them in a neighborhood store. I got into crack, and my drug problem went out of control. I overdosed several times and had to go to the hospital. My mother got me into a drug rehabilitation program. I am now eighteen trying to stay away from crack."

Not too much in the way of reliable behavior can be expected from crack addicts. They are poor decision-makers because they cannot think clearly or focus their thoughts. They cannot concentrate, they learn poorly, and as a consequence they drop out of school. They are drug-dependent and therefore must use devious means such as lying, cheating, stealing, drug dealing, and prostitution to get the money to buy crack. They destroy family relationships because their behavior is not compatible with family living, which requires that each member bear some responsibility for the well-being of the group. Some crack abusers resort to crime and violence. Many, reaching the depths of despair, attempt to take their own lives. Some are successful in this final act of violence.

HOW CRACK-ADDICTED TEENS CAN BE HELPED

The administrator of a cocaine hot line, Richard Jensen, advises that users who wish to be rehabilitated or people concerned about them should contact a drug problem center, a counselor, or a physician. It is important to get a mental health professional involved. He advises further that a person concerned about a teen who uses crack should do the following:

- Confront the teen with the problem. If the addiction is ignored, it will get worse.
- Let the teen know that the problem is treatable and that there are ways to get help. Be supportive, but firm.
- Be sure not to "facilitate the abuse" by using drugs or supplying unlimited amounts of money. Do not assume that the problem is "normal adolescent behavior." It will simply get worse.

Peers must be aware that crack is dangerous. It hooks its users faster than any of the other drugs and makes them more dangerous. Violent paranoia is a common effect of crack use. Drug expert Dr. Armand DiMele says that crack "significantly alters brain chemistry. The intense paranoia induced by crack produces exaggerated fears and delusions in people's minds. Everybody becomes a user's potential enemies. He strikes first to get them before they can get him."

A SAD TWIST TO THE CRACK STORY

The newspaper account that follows tells the story:

CRACK-HOOKED BABIES
ZOOMING IN NUMBER
The number of babies born addicted to crack has skyrocketed this year [1987], straining the city's already overtaxed foster-care system, officials reported recently.

Eric Brettschneider, who heads the city Special Services for Children Division, said 401 addicted infants were born in the three months ended June 30, up 161% from 151 in the previous year period.

You know that cocaine dissolves in the blood and travels to all parts of the body. Cocaine diffuses through the placenta in the pregnant uterus and then into the bloodstream of the developing embryo. Babies are born just as addicted to crack as their addicted mothers. These mothers are usually unmarried teenagers who accept little responsibility for their drug-addicted babies. Most of them abandon the babies, leaving them in the hospital as charges of the city welfare agency.

These babies require special care. Most of them are brain-damaged. Many suffer other abnormalities such as damaged hearts. The large number of these babies, drug-addicted, abandoned, and sick, have come to be known as "boarder" babies because they remain in the hospitals with no home to take them in.

This is indeed a sad story, but one that will be repeated hundreds of times over as long as crack is easily available to drug-abusing persons of child-bearing age.

ANOTHER TWIST TO THE CRACK STORY

Drug abusers are always seeking the perfect high. Crack provides the user with an intense high that lasts from eight to ten minutes. In that time span, crack users seem to experience very pleasurable feelings. However, when the high wears off users are left in an extreme state of anxiety. They become jittery and depressed. Their only relief is to smoke more crack, continuing the cycle of smoking, euphoria, crash. The underground drug chemists are always at work mixing their wares of destruction, as illustrated in a newspaper account:

NEW CRACK MIXTURE ON THE STREETS LURES YOUNG GENERATION TO HEROIN

Drug-treatment officials are worried about a highly addictive mixture of crack and a smokable heroin that is being sold to drug abusers in New York City. The new mixture of crack and heroin is smoked in a pipe. The smokable heroin lengthens the time of the crack high and reduces the intensity of the depressions that follow it. The mixture is very dangerous because it doubly addicts users to both drugs, crack and heroin, and leaves them in a state of chronic intoxication. The high from heroin, a sedative, may last as long as four hours. Addicts who use this mixture are getting the worst of both drugs. The treatment of addicts with this double addiction is very difficult. Treatment specialists fear that using the smokable form of heroin will lure a younger group of users and will eventually lead them to use injectable heroin. Lisa, a 28-year-old crack addict under treatment, summed up the use of the new mixture by saying, "A lot of people are chasing the dragon now." "Chasing the dragon" is an old term newly applied to smoking heroin with crack.

Comedian/actor John Belushi died as a result of injecting himself with a mixture of heroin and cocaine. This injectable mixture was known as "speedball." Addicts are now calling the smokable version of heroin and crack "speedball" and "crank," names given to other street drugs, but used differently. Because the new mixture of crack and heroin is smoked in a pipe, it may be more appealing to women and teenagers than intravenous injections. Drug treatment officials fear that the new mixture may attract an increasing number of users.

SUMMARY

Crack is a new deadly form of cocaine, a new menace to society. On the West Coast it is called "rock" because it resembles small chips of stone. No matter the name, crack is more addictive and destructive of body and mind than most other drugs sold on the street.

Crack is made from cocaine hydrochloride, freed from its base. Crack is almost pure cocaine transformed for smoking. The effects of crack reach the brain in six minutes; the high lasts no longer than ten minutes. The user is then

plunged into a deep and desperate depression, so great that many users attempt suicide. Many abusers become mentally deranged and violent on crack. The increase in violence by crack addicts is both alarming and overwhelming. Robberies and killings have become a way of life for addicts who must have a ready supply of money for another "hit" and another...Crack is smoked continuously until money or the drug is gone.

A woman poured gasoline on her husband and lit the fuel, burning him to death because he had urged her to get treatment for her crack addiction.

HELP CAN BE OBTAINED FOR CRACK ADDICTION

A twenty-four-hour national referral and information service about crack and cocaine can be reached by calling 1-800-COCAINE. In New York State help can be obtained by calling 1-800-522-5353.

Write the National Federation of Parents for Drug-Free Youth, 8730 Georgia Avenue, Silver Spring, MD 20910, or call 1-800-544-KIDS for information.

Crack addiction does not go away by ignoring it; it only gets worse. Because crack is so destructive to the addict and to others, immediate help should be sought.

CHAPTER 8

Crack Destroys People and Places

It was three o'clock in the morning. Rickey was sitting astride his bicycle in a place where the neighborhood crack dealers plied their awful trade. Rickey was not without his family. His crack-dealer older brother and crackhead mother were standing nearby when a dispute erupted between rival drug gangs. Rickey was killed by a stray bullet that struck him between the eyes. The short life of Rickey Clark was over: eleven years old, school dropout, drug-runner, and lookout.

CRACK AND VIOLENCE: THE SOURCE

Crack and violence go hand in hand. They are hopelessly linked. Where there is crack, there is violence. Over the

past few years, the dramatic increase in violent crimes across the country has been attributed to the sale and use of crack.

The violence of crack begins in the coca fields of Colombia, Peru, and Bolivia. These South American countries are the largest producers of cocaine in the world. Colombia is the center of refining and processing of cocaine for export and therefore makes much more money from the drug than its smaller and poorer neighbors.

The drug trade in Colombia is run by two tightly structured organizations called *cartels*. These cartels, known as Medellin and Cali for the cities in which they operate, are really merchants of death. Not only is the product that they grow, refine, and smuggle into the United States a destroyer of people, but also the cartels hire and train professional assassins who kill anyone who threatens their operations.

The Colombian cartels have declared war on law-enforcement agents who attempt to interrupt their drug business. Within a few short months eighty judges and other law-enforcement officials were killed, but the killing is not confined to Colombia. More than a dozen Colombian nationals were killed in the United States. The heads of the cartels have threatened death to any law-enforcement agent, whether in Colombia or the United States, who challenges their activities.

CRACK AND VIOLENCE IN U.S. CITIES

Crack, the smokable form of cocaine, has become the drug of choice in the inner cities. With uncanny efficiency and cunning, dealers in the cities have organized their operations so that street sales of crack are handled by juvenile dealers. These young people are organized into crack gangs

that control their territories with a ruthlessness that has no match in the history of American crime. More heavily armed than the police, gang members shoot to kill anyone, policeman or civilian, who threatens their drug dealing. Gangs like the Los Angeles "Bloods" and "Crips" or the East Coast Jamaican "posses" have as members preteen-agers, teenagers, and young adults numbering more than 200,000. The lives of the gang members themselves are threatened by the drug and by the mindless violence that accompanies crack dealing.

Crack gang members are always at shooting war with rival gangs and with each other. People caught in the cross-fire are innocent victims of a system that is seemingly uncontrollable:

- A nineteen-year-old woman was killed while using a pay phone in the Bronx, New York.
- A four-year-old boy was killed in the crossfire of a gang shootout in Brooklyn, New York.
- A man sitting up in bed was killed by a stray bullet that crashed through his window during a gang fight on an adjacent rooftop in the Bronx, New York.
- In Queens, New York, a woman holding her baby was shot to death by four men who fired eighteen bullets into her home, having mistaken it for the home of a rival drug dealer.
- Los Angeles experiences wanton killings of by-standers and malicious killings of innocent people who are sprayed with bullets as drug dealers drive through neighborhoods proclaiming their power over their turf.
- A woman in Washington, DC, was killed while standing in line to enter a disco—caught in the middle of a shootout.

Both traffickers (those who move cocaine into the United States) and dealers use unmerciful violence to continue their operations. Violence is present in every phase of the drug trade from the coca fields in South America to the streets of North America, in cities, small towns, and suburbs.

CRACK DESTROYS PEOPLE

A recent survey carried out by the National Parents' Resource Institute for Drug Education (PRIDE) indicates that one percent of 6th graders in the United States have used cocaine. Approximately 400,000 junior high school students at 958 schools nationwide were surveyed about drug and alcohol use. Cocaine use among eleven-year-olds had never been surveyed before. It has been reported that in Harlem (New York) nine-year-old youngsters are hooked on crack.

Crack destroys people in a number of ways. It turns users into instruments of destruction. Mark Walker is an example. Crazed on crack, he killed his grandmother and then jumped out of a window. Maria Hernandez was killed because she worked with her husband to drive the crack dealers and addicts from their neighborhood. Crackheads in hospitals attack medical personnel who try to assist them through the agony of the crack crash.

Crack is destroying families. In the poorest inner-city neighborhoods, most families are headed by single mothers who struggle to keep their family intact. The appearance of crack in ghetto neighborhoods has brought devastation to many of these families when the female head-of-household has become a crack user. Crack-addicted mothers harm their children: use the food money for drugs, do violence to children, and spend their days on the streets looking for the next hit.

To support their always increasing craving for crack, many women become involved in robbery or prostitution. Eventually, women who steal to support their drug habit are caught and jailed, and their youngsters are put into foster homes. Crack is responsible for drastically increasing the numbers of neglected and abandoned children who have overloaded the foster-care system in New York City. In a period of three months ending June 30, 1989, 401 infants addicted to crack were born in the city. Many addicted infants are left in the hospitals by the mothers and become the so-called "boarder babies," children both destroyed and abandoned by drug-addicted mothers.

The breakdown of services is apparent in most government agencies that exist to serve the ghetto areas of large cities. Women seeking help for their addiction are turned away from treatment centers because there is no room. The cycle continues: addicted mother, addicted and abandoned baby.

Women who engage in prostitution to support their crack habit add another burden to their children. Over the course of a year in New York City, the number of babies born addicted to cocaine totaled more than 6,000. Babies born infected with AIDS and syphilis are ever-increasing.

CRACK AND AIDS DESTROY BABIES

Mothers in poor neighborhoods are becoming increasingly addicted to crack. When the pregnant mother smokes crack, cocaine vapors pass through the placenta and into the bloodstream and tissues of the fetus. Cocaine's effect on the fetus and newborn is devastating. It diffuses into brain cells, destroying some that control learning and behavior. Cocaine can damage the heart muscle of the fetus, insuring a defective heart in the newborn. Cocaine-exposed and -addicted babies are underweight, likely to die before birth or shortly thereafter, or suffer an array of physical disabilities that will remain with them for life.

Imagine the torture of addiction that a cocaine baby suffers. The pain of withdrawal is just as terrible as in teenagers and adults, but cocaine-addicted babies are fragile. Their nervous system becomes overloaded easily. They are hypersensitive and irritable, screaming without letup at the slightest noise or change in position. Most of these children will have learning and personality problems for life.

Crack destroys babies in other ways. Many crack-addicted pregnant mothers carry in their bloodstream HIV, the virus of AIDS. In poverty pockets throughout large cities, the death rate for babies is rising. Detroit and Washington have 21 deaths for each 1,000 live births. In Harlem, in New York, the infant mortality rate is 27.6 per 1,000 live births; in the Fort Green section of Brooklyn it is 19.5. These babies die from AIDS infection, drug addiction, or a combination of both. AIDS is an infectious disease that shuts down the immune system of the infected person. Addicted women contract the virus through sexual contacts and pass it to the fetus. AIDS infection kills women more quickly than it does men; infected women die shortly after giving birth, leaving behind orphaned children.

CRACK DESTROYS COMMUNITIES

We have said that crack and other drug usage increases crime. In a recent study, drug tests were made on men arrested in fourteen major cities. The table shows the percentages of drug-using suspects. Most of the men tested had been arrested for burglary. More than half of the men arrested for murder tested positive for a particular drug. Among women tested, those testing positive for drug use ranged from 80 percent in San Diego to 45 percent in St. Louis. In New York, women's use of cocaine was greater than men's.

City	Percentage
Chicago	78%
New Orleans	75
Portland, Ore.	70
Birmingham	70
Detroit	69
Cleveland	68
Dallas	57
Phoenix	57
St. Louis	56

There is no doubt that the drug trade is ruining neighborhoods. Nearly 2,000 residents of the Bedford-Stuyvesant section of Brooklyn took what they called a "crack walk." Escorted by the police, these community people and their clergy walked through areas where the drug trafficking is heavy. At each drug-selling location the walkers stopped and the clergy led them in a short ecumenical prayer service. Community activity such as this puts the drug dealers and their customers on notice that the many decent people in the neighborhood are aware of their actions and do not like them.

The "crack house" is a horrible kind of place that has come into being in crack-infested areas. Usually, it is an abandoned house where crack dealers sell the drug, crackheads smoke it, and many violent misdeeds occur. In neighborhoods where there were no abandoned houses, crack dealers have driven people out of their apartments and ruthlessly set up shop. Afraid of being killed, the displaced tenants have been known to offer little resistance.

St. David's Church in the Bronx, New York, formed a coalition of churches that took action to have a crack house removed from the neighborhood. Invoking a federal law that permits the seizing of property where drugs are sold, the police had the six-story apartment house demolished.

Throughout the country, community residents are banding together to drive out the drug dealers. In Philadelphia three churches of different denominations joined together to take back a park from the drug dealers. The Muslims in a Brooklyn neighborhood drove the dealers from several crack houses and warned them not to return.

Crack ruins neighborhoods. Crack addicts children, women, and men. Addicted people steal, mug, and sell drugs to get money to feed an increasing habit. Crack dealers fill a neighborhood with the dregs of humanity, making it unsafe for normal people. The hospitals become overloaded with addicts and those who are shot in drug wars. In some areas, so many hospital beds are taken up by addicts that there are not enough for nonaddicted sick persons. Schools in crack-infested areas become the sites of drug sales and gang violence.

Crack is moving from the inner city to the suburbs. Dr. Jeffrey S. Rosecan, who heads the cocaine abuse center at New York's Columbia-Presbyterian Medical Center, says that crack is proving to be just as addictive among the middle class. "Only it's more behind closed doors in nice homes." Bill Coonce, who heads the Detroit office of the Drug Enforcement Administration, says: "It's not just a black or minority drug. We're seeing a rapid expansion of addiction now into suburban and small-town America."

Tom S. was an assembly-line worker making $35,000 a year. He, his wife, and children lived in their own home in the suburbs. One day at work Tom was introduced to cocaine by a fellow worker. His use of cocaine continued on a weekly basis for a while. Then he began using it twice a week, then daily. From snorting cocaine, he moved to smoking crack. The habit became so expensive that he not only spent all his earnings but also borrowed against his house to support his drug use. Ultimately, Tom lost his job, his house, and his family. He now drifts in the city streets in the population of addicted homeless.

SUMMARY

Crack is not a fun drug; no drug is. Crack is a drug that addicts, destroys minds, devastates neighborhoods, and brings with it a fury of violence that this nation has never before seen. Children who have not yet reached their teens are involved in crack sales; kids as young as nine are becoming addicted. Women addicted to crack are giving birth to cocaine-addicted babies, many of whom are also infected with the sexually transmitted disease AIDS.

Crack addicts live in the cities and suburbs. Males, females, people of all races and ethnic groups, young children and young adults, and even some mid-thirties people are destroying their lives. Murders increase alarmingly as crack spreads.

A word of caution. Crack addiction is not easily cured. It is a long, hard, painful, and expensive process that not only involves initial hospitalization but also years of psychotherapy. Not enough treatment services are available to poor people and never will be. The increase in addicted persons has become explosive. All of the financial resources of city and state governments could be used just on treatment for crack addicts. Most die from overdose, heart attack, or murder.

Don't get caught in the crack trap. Don't take the first cocaine snort or crack smoke. It will not be your last. Remember, there is no escape from crack addiction, its violence, and personal devastation.

CHAPTER 9

Sniffing Volatile

Substances

WHO ARE THE SNIFFERS?

Studies indicate that youngsters who turn to sniffing usually come from disorganized homes. This has nothing to do with rich or poor, race or religion. But it has a great deal to do with the personal relationships within the home. Where families are torn by strife, disturbed adolescents often turn to sniffing, alone or with a group, as a means of problem-solving.

Glue-sniffers, like all other drug users, try to conceal the practice. But there are certain indications of glue-sniffing. Following is a list of signs and symptoms of abuse:

running nose	watering eyes
chemical odor on clothing	staggering
chemical odor on breath	uncertain gait
poor muscular control	slurred speech
double vision	drowsiness
foul breath	plastic bag evidence

It must also be noted that while intoxicated, glue-sniffers tend toward committing violent acts against themselves. Repeated use seems to increase the self-violence.

Tommy R. was fourteen years old, small for his age and seemingly very quiet. But on the inside he was a seething cauldron of hatred. His only "friend" and constant companion was a switch-blade knife, which he used frequently and surreptitiously. He stabbed viciously at the desks and chairs in classrooms. He maliciously hacked sizable pieces of cork from the hallway bulletin boards. He dug gaping holes in the wall plaster in the boys' rooms and scraped the enamel from the drinking fountains. Tommy's knife not only slashed away at wood and cork and plaster. If you rolled up his sleeves and looked at his arms you could see that at times Tommy turned the knife against himself. Tommy was a glue-sniffer.

WHAT HAPPENS TO GLUE-SNIFFERS?

They die from suffocation or organ destruction; or they undergo rehabilitation as a result of arrest and court order or the person's own desire; or they move on to hard drugs, usually heroin.

ADULTS ARE SNIFFERS, TOO

On the street they are called poppers. Street vendors sell amyl or butyl nitrate in ampules or in bottles, openly and aggressively. These chemicals are legal. At one time amyl nitrate was used as a cardiac stimulant for angina patients; now it is used by "high" seekers. Butyl nitrate has no medicinal use but is marketed as a room deodorizer.

Adult devotees of disco dancing seem to be devoted to sniffing butyl nitrate and its cousin isobutyl nitrate. (Amyl nitrate is now more difficult to get.) Inhalation produces a rapid heartbeat and flushed face, as the mind-altering drug acts to dilate blood vessels and to decrease blood pressure. Disco dancers say they enjoy the way poppers intensify the rhythm of the music.

"Some people get really excessive," said one twenty-six-year-old, who himself inhales ten to twenty times during an evening of disco dancing. "I don't like it when you get to the point where you can't stand up. I've thought about negative effects, but it's not enough to stop me from doing it...."

The high from butyl nitrate can be followed by headaches, nausea, vomiting, dizziness, and fainting.

The State of Connecticut has banned its sale outright. Some drug and mental health experts and doctors hope that butyl nitrate is just a passing fad. It is hoped that no deaths will occur from the misuse of these substances.

SUMMARY

The sniffing of volatile substances is a kind of drug abuse against which it is difficult to pass legislation. The adolescent prone to glue-sniffing will use any common volatile household chemical to produce intoxication. The kind of young person who turns to this means of stimulation is emotionally unstable and needs the help of trained counselors to direct his energies to more productive goals.

Glue-sniffing and the sniffing of any chemical is a dangerous practice because vital body organs are destroyed. In addition, intoxication from fumes usually drives the young person to commit horrible acts against himself.

Why become involved?

CHAPTER 10

Alcohol, the Legal Intoxicant

ALCOHOL AS A WAY OF LIFE

An alcoholic is a person who cannot drink alcoholic beverages in moderation. He or she drinks excessively to the point of intoxication. We say that an alcoholic suffers from alcoholism, a disease that drives a person to drink beyond the point of functioning. Not all problem drinkers are "Skid Row" bums. It is estimated that at least five million Americans abuse alcohol to the stage of intoxication. You can understand that a person who drinks excessively is a problem not only to himself but also to his family and his community.

George is a seventeen-year-old high school freshman. Although the other pupils in his classes are much younger, he does not seem out of place because of his short stature and thin physique. George has a ten-block walk from the bus stop to school. To shorten the distance and to gain a little privacy, he cuts across the cemetery that is adjacent to his school. However, if you were to watch George on his morning walk, you would notice that in addition to his books he carries a brown paper bag that hardly masks the bottle inside. Every once in a while George stops, puts the bottle to his lips, and takes a few gulping swigs. As long as George has his wine, he can "make it" through the school day. His stumps of broken teeth do not hurt him so much, and those cranky teachers don't "bug" him. George has been drinking since the age of twelve.

A BIT OF HISTORY

Probably as long as humans have been on earth, they have made and consumed alcohol. It might have been by accident that the uncivilized human learned to ferment grain, leaves, and fruits to make a drink that could relax or intoxicate. Clay tablets dug from a Mesopotamian mound dating from 3000 B.C. indicate that beer was regarded as a staple. The tomb inscriptions of ancient Egyptian pharaohs show that alcohol was part of the daily ration.

Whether civilized or not, each culture group has given alcohol a prominent place in its religious or social practices. As far back as the first century A.D., the Roman statesman Pliny the Elder declared that "in no part of the world is drunkenness ever at a loss." The sixteenth-century explorers of Mexico discovered and sampled fermented essence of maguey leaves, known today as tequila. The eighteenth-century explorers of the Polynesian Islands enjoyed to excess the stimulating kava, fermented from sweet peppers. The nineteenth-century explorers of the Sahara region imbibed a kind of beer made by the African tribesmen. And so the story of man's use of alcohol goes on into modern times. There is hardly a country today where alcohol is not used.

PROHIBITION

To prevent alcoholism, a thirteen-year "experiment" known as Prohibition was enacted into law. The Eighteenth Amendment to the Constitution, which became effective in 1920, made the manufacture and sale of alcoholic beverages illegal in the United States. This "dry" period did not prevent alcoholism. Instead, it made fortunes for underworld liquor manufacturers and dealers known as "bootleggers." Illicitly made products endangered the lives of the drinking public by forcing them to buy alcoholic beverages that were not subject to government controls for quality and purity.

Along with bootlegging came vicious crimes. Gangsters fought for the control of the lucrative alcohol market, plunging the United States into an era of wholesale murders and gangland wars. Because an alcohol embargo was not the answer to excessive drinking, the Twenty-first Amendment to the Constitution repealed the Prohibition Act. Alcohol was once again manufactured, sold, and consumed legally in most places. However, there remain some small towns throughout the United States that still have prohibition laws.

WHAT ALCOHOL IS

Alcohol is a compound with the chemical formula C_2H_5OH. It is made by a process called *fermentation*. When yeasts are placed in a medium of sugar and water under conditions of reduced air and warmth, they become biochemically active. Not only do these one-celled fungi grow and reproduce, but also they give off an enzyme known as zymase. Zymase aids in the partial chemical breakdown of sugar molecules into alcohol and carbon dioxide.

Alcohol is a colorless, volatile, inflammable liquid. It has a sharp odor and a penetrating taste. When alcohol is made from grain, it is called ethyl alcohol, a product not toxic to humans. Methyl alcohol or wood alcohol is not drinkable because it is poisonous to living tissue. This type of alcohol is used for industrial purposes. Denatured alcohol is ethyl alcohol that has been treated with poisons to render it unfit for drinking but useful for laboratory and industrial work.

Alcoholic beverages are classified by a strength rating known as *proof*. The proof is computed by doubling the percentage of alcohol in the beverage. For example, the percentage of pure alcohol is 100; its proof is 200. One hundred proof rum has an alcoholic content of 50 percent.

Kinds of Alcoholic Beverages

Name of drink	Produced by action of yeast on	Alcoholic content
beer	grain	4–5%
ale	malt and hops	6–8%
wines	juices of fruits	10–14%
gin	grain flavored with juniper berries*	45%
rum	cane sugar syrup*	50%
brandy	fruits*	43%
vodka	wheat flavored with malt*	72%
whiskey	starchy grains such as corn, rye*	45%
tequila	maguey leaves*	50%

* followed by distillation

ALCOHOL PATHWAYS

What happens within the body when a person drinks alcohol? Ultimately, it is transported to the brain by way of the bloodstream. But the effects of alcohol vary because of the multiple conditions that alter its pathway through the digestive system into the bloodstream and then on to the brain.

In general, the effects of alcohol are modified by a person's physical condition, his or her tolerance, temperament, food habits, and drinking preference. These conditions in turn determine others:

1. The route that alcohol takes to reach the bloodstream.
2. The speed at which alcohol travels.
3. Other substances that alcohol meets in the digestive system.

Alcohol travels from the mouth to the stomach. There, absorption takes place, emptying small quantities of alcohol into the blood. Dilute drinks such as beer (4 percent alcohol) or highballs (20 percent alcohol) are absorbed very slowly. Most of the alcohol in a beverage is absorbed rather rapidly in the small intestine. However, proteins and fats slow absorption. Therefore, people who eat while drinking decrease the speed with which alcohol reaches the circulatory system. Russians are able to drink large quantities of potent vodka (72 percent alcohol) because they eat great mouthfuls of foods rich in fats and proteins: caviar, sausage, and herring.

You may have heard people say that they can handle straight whiskey better than mixed drinks. There are reasons for that. High-proof drinks pass into the bloodstream more slowly than dilute ones. The pyloric sphincter, the valve that regulates the passage of substances from the stomach to the small intestine, is sensitive to high alcohol concentrations. The sphincter closes when touched by strong alcohol. This, of course, delays absorption in the small intestine. Conversely, carbon dioxide relaxes the pyloric sphincter, causing it to open. This in effect speeds up the passage of drinks from the stomach into the intestine, resulting in quick absorption. Thus alcohol in carbonated drinks such as highballs and champagne reaches the bloodstream rather rapidly.

ALCOHOL AND BODY PHYSIOLOGY

Contrary to popular belief, alcohol is not a stimulant. It is a depressant. Alcohol's target organ is the brain; its action within the brain is selective. This drug depresses the reticular formation. As a result, faulty messages are sent to the cerebral cortex, the cerebellum, and the medulla. The amount of signal distortion that occurs depends upon the drink, the drinker, and the circumstances under which the drinking takes place. In varying degrees alcohol consumption causes mental disorganization, slurred speech, staggering gait, sleep, coma, or death.

The degree to which alcohol changes behavior is directly related to the amounts reaching the bloodstream. The table that follows shows why the concentration of alcohol in the blood is important to the drinker.

As you can see, a high percentage of alcohol in the blood has an immediate effect on the cerebral cortex. It makes this region of the brain function in an erratic and disorganized way. The personality of a drinker changes. He suffers some memory loss, and his ability to make construc-

Percentage of alcohol in the blood	Levels of intoxication
.05	Intoxication Begins
.10	affects behavior reduces inhibitions causes slurred speech affects equilibrium
.12	New Law Definition of Under the Influence of Alcohol
.15	Traditional Definition of Legal Intoxication
.20	slows reflexes impairs judgment causes staggering causes incoherent speech
.30	makes one unable to stand
.40	renders one unconscious
.50–.60	results in death

tive judgments is impaired. The mood swings. A mood that may be expansive and vivacious one minute can dip to depression the next. What other drugs cause similar mood changes?

Alcohol is quite a thorough depressant. It inhibits the involuntary center in the brain that controls the expanding and contracting of blood vessels. In response to alcohol, the capillaries dilate and are able to hold more blood. More blood in these small blood vessels means that more internal heat is carried to the skin and thence dissipated. The dilation of capillaries is responsible for the red noses and flushed faces of regular drinkers. The seemingly warm body of the drinker is an illusion. In reality, body temperature falls. Many vagrants die in cold weather because of the sudden and dangerous body chilling brought on by alcohol. For the same reason, drinking a rum punch under the tropical sun is cooling.

To some extent, kidney function is controlled by a portion of the brain's medulla. The inhibitory effect of alcohol prevents the kidney tubules from working efficiently. Instead of reabsorbing large amounts of water, the tubules permit water loss. Thus the drinker is often faced with the problem of frequent urination. It is not unusual for an intoxicated person to lose the ability to hold his water.

HOW ALCOHOL LEAVES THE BODY

As blood circulates through the body, one of its pathways leads to the liver. In this gland alcohol is metabolized in an orderly process. First the liver filters alcohol out of the blood. Then at a slow steady rate liver enzymes aid in the conversion of alcohol to acetaldehyde. In a fraction of a second this very toxic acetaldehyde is changed to acetic acid, which is discharged from the liver into the blood. The blood then carries the acetic acid to the body cells, where it is oxidized. During oxidation, chemical energy is wrung from each acetic acid molecule, leaving the waste products of carbon dioxide and water. Note: alcohol does provide the body with calories, but it contains no vitamins.

If alcohol is destroyed by the liver and the body cells, how then is it able to affect the brain? The answer to this question depends upon rate and time. The liver can handle only one quarter of an ounce of alcohol per hour. This amount is equivalent to half a jigger glass. Alcohol consumed at a faster rate remains in the blood. As the blood

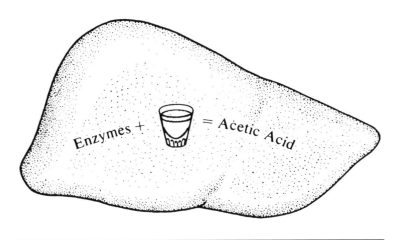

How fast can the liver process each jigger glass of alcohol?

circulates, alcohol depresses the brain centers until it can be processed by the liver. An outcome of excessive drinking is cirrhosis of the liver, a cancer condition, which kills the victim.

CHRONIC ALCOHOLISM AND DT'S

Alcoholism is a ruthless disease, responsible for damage to the body organs and to the mind. A constant threat to the chronic alcoholic is sudden withdrawal from the drug. One complication resulting from sudden withdrawal is delirium tremens, commonly called DT's. Death claims about 15 percent of those who experience DT's because of the shock or circulatory collapse that follows the extremely high fevers that accompany the disease.

The effects of alcohol are wide-ranging and differ among alcoholics. Perhaps this is due to difference in body chemistry or to nutritional habits. Researchers do not agree on the causes of alcoholism or its effects. However, some alcoholics never experience DT's; others have repeated bouts. Delirium tremens may be caused by altered brain function brought about by alcohol abuse. It occurs in those who have been excessive and steady drinkers over a period of years. It may also occur after a drinking binge. Current research suggests that DT's results from a biochemical disorder in the brain.

There are definite signs of the onset of DT's in an alcoholic or drug abuser. The person experiences hallucinations that usually involve insects, spiders, or other bugs, which seem to have missing legs. It is also imagined that animals are in the room, probably caused by a misinterpretation of shadows and sounds. The person in delirium talks compulsively and indistinctly. The arms and legs shake because of muscle twitches and spasms. All of these symptoms are accompanied by fever, which may be high enough (107°F) to cause collapse of the circulatory system.

Doctors consider DT's to be a medical emergency. The victim is given large amounts of water intravenously. The ions of sodium, potassium, and magnesium are added to the fluid feeding to replace those lost in the perspiration that occurs with high fever. The muscle tremors are treated with tranquilizing drugs such as Valium, Librium, Thorazine, or Compazine. Attacks of DT's end as abruptly as they began, in about two days.

ALCOHOL AND THE PREGNANT MOTHER

There is growing evidence that moderate drinking on two or three occasions during pregnancy may cause lasting damage to an unborn child. Recently pediatricians discovered that children of chronic alcoholic mothers may be born with what has come to be known as "fetal alcohol syndrome," a group of about twenty defects including small head size, mental retardation, slow development, and abnormalities of the face and skeleton. Several studies have shown that one ounce of alcohol a day, the amount in two highballs or three beers, is capable of causing subtle defects in newborns such as trembling and decreased alertness.

It is advisable for pregnant mothers not to drink. Alcohol can affect the unborn child in different ways. In the first three months of the developing embryo alcohol can destroy the central nervous system, damage the brain, affect the circulatory system, and adversely affect another system that is developing at this time. Alcohol interferes with the growth of the developing fetus during the second trimester (three-month period) of pregnancy. This may be because alcohol drinking by the mother diminishes the supply of nutrients and vitamins that are available to the baby. Alcohol consumption and pregnancy do not mix.

THE SOCIAL SIGNIFICANCE OF ALCOHOL

The sentences that follow are taken from a recent newspaper article.

"According to the National Safety Council, one out of every 50 drivers is driving under the influence of alcohol. Alcohol is indicated as a factor in at least half of all fatal motor vehicle accidents in the United States. . . ."

In addition to highway deaths, people under the influence of alcohol are responsible for the increasing number of industrial accidents, crimes of violence against adults and against children, housebreaking and robbery, and welfare recipients. Recently a study was made of 2,816 family units receiving child welfare assistance. This study excluded families in which there was only one parent and children in foster homes. It was found that 21.8 percent of these families have a history of problem drinkers identified as follows: fathers, 59.0 percent; mothers, 25.8 percent; juveniles 15.2 percent.

Currently a new and alarming twist is being added to the alcohol story. The number of juvenile alcoholics seems to be increasing. Along with this increase in juvenile and teenage drinking is a sharp increase in the number of highway fatalities caused by driving under the influence of alcohol. Several states are trying to reduce these fatalities by raising the drinking age. The federal government and many states are considering raising the legal drinking age to 21. A further turn of events is that many young drinkers are using alcohol in combination with other drugs.

There is great social significance to alcohol use. It is used as part of religious rituals, in celebrations, and as a table beverage. Not every one who takes a drink is a problem drinker or an alcoholic. Most people in the population are not troubled by the need to abuse alcohol.

The *occasional drinker* is one who drinks on rare occasions. Even then, this person drinks sparingly. He or she is not committed to alcohol in daily life, and it would not bother the occasional drinker if there were no access to liquor. For this type of drinker, alcohol is never a problem.

The *frequent drinker* is one who might be classified as a "social drinker." This person takes a few drinks at parties and social gatherings because it gives him a good feeling. A person in this group never drinks enough to get drunk and does not become an alcoholic because alcohol is not used as a problem-solver.

The *regular drinker* is one for whom drinking is an

important part of everyday life. For this type of person, the cocktail or "shot of whiskey" is a vital part of lunch. So is the little "pick-me-up" before dinner important to his feelings of well-being. A drinker who fits this category does not use alcohol to the point of intoxication and could give up drinking if the reason were compelling enough.

The *heavy drinker* is a person to whom alcohol becomes a problem. This person is alcohol-dependent. He or she cannot enjoy an event without drinking, nor can anxiety situations be met without resorting to alcohol. Heavy drinkers use alcohol excessively for all occasions: pleasure, problem-solving, relaxation. Persons in this category drink too much and at times become intoxicated. They cannot give up alcohol without great difficulty. Heavy drinkers can become alcoholics.

Alcoholics are drinkers who have lost control over the consumption of alcohol. Their drinking is chronic; it gets continually worse and leads to intoxication. Alcoholics are so preoccupied with alcohol that they cannot function in an occupational setting, socially, or emotionally without it. In the late stages of alcoholism, many alcoholics lose interest in food. They do not eat and become emaciated. Alcoholism is probably caused by a complex interaction of several factors: psychological, physiological, sociological, and even economic. These factors can set off in a person who is alcohol-prone a set of behaviors that leads to chronic alcoholism.

HELP FOR THE ALCOHOLIC

Alcohol is one of this country's worst drug problems. There are about 10 million alcohol abusers, including the 1.13 million school children between the ages of twelve and seventeen who get drunk at least once a week. Sixty percent of all moving-vehicle accidents are caused by drunk drivers. Alcohol and driving do not mix. Alcohol not only slows reaction time but also makes a person unusually aggressive, causing him to take chances that he would not otherwise take. It has been estimated that 205,000 deaths a year are alcohol-related. Half of the homicides committed and one-third of the suicides are related to alcohol use.

Because alcohol is such a major problem in the United States, at least two-thirds of the states have some kind of community-directed alcohol education program. Although the programs offered in each state differ, they have two common features. One is to prevent alcoholism. The other is to provide help for the alcoholic. It is difficult to assess the success of these programs. The number of alcoholics continues to grow.

Alcoholics Anonymous is a private program that was founded by two alcoholics, a physician and a stockbroker, in 1935. More than any other agency, it has been successful in helping people find their way back to sobriety. Although no records of attendance, abstinence, or relapse to former drug habits are kept, the success of AA is estimated at above 50 percent. Any alcoholic can join an AA group. He or she needs only an honest desire to stop drinking.

The "drug-free" programs established for the treatment of drug addicts have based their methods on those used by AA. Nonprofessional workers, former alcoholics, try to imbue active alcoholics with feelings of dignity and spiritual awakening. Through individual and group counseling, problem drinkers are helped to gain a foothold on life.

OTHER PROGRAMS

The problem of alcoholism is complex. A variety of inter-acting factors cause a person to become alcohol-dependent. An important part of treatment centers about the emotional problems of the alcoholic and the capability of their being untangled. Help in this direction is provided not only in the counseling situation, but is needed at home also. The family of the alcoholic must be able to render support and understanding.

Al-Anon is an organization for the nondrinking spouse of the alcoholic. The purpose of this group is to help the sober partner to understand alcoholism and to learn how he or she can help the spouse fight the battle against alcohol.

Alateen is an organization for the teenage children of alcoholics. The purpose of this group is to provide under-standing through group counseling sessions so that young people can help in the support treatment of an alcoholic parent.

SUMMARY

For some people alcohol is a relaxer; for others, an intoxi-cant. It is not known why alcohol affects some people so severely that they become alcoholics. The problems of the alcoholic touch upon and become interwoven with all phases of daily life. The alcoholic presents a medical prob-lem, a family problem, a political problem, a financial problem, an educational problem. Recognition of the alco-holic as an ill person is not enough. Concerted effort must be made by communities to prevent alcoholism through viable educational programs and to treat and rehabilitate alcoholics.

Is king-size safer?

CHAPTER 11

Tobacco, the Legal Carcinogen

A SHORT HISTORY OF TOBACCO USAGE

For how long the Indians of the Americas had been growing and using tobacco prior to the discovery of the New World is not known. The sixteenth-century explorers carried back with them to Europe the "American Indian herb" that could be smoked. One such explorer was Francisco Fernandes, who in 1558 introduced tobacco into Spain. In 1585 Sir Francis Drake took the tobacco weed to England. The popularity of tobacco increased through the writings of Jean Nicot, French ambassador to Portugal (1560), who praised the herb for its curative powers. With little introductions here and there, the use of tobacco spread throughout Europe and Asia.

Worldwide, there are only two species of tobacco. *Nicotiana rustica*, a wild species, is grown in the Soviet Union, Asia, and Europe. It has no commercial value in the United States because its smoke is too harsh and biting.

The only species grown in the U.S. is *Nicotiana tabacum.*
Its leaves yield a lighter, pleasanter, more mellow smoke.

Before the twentieth century tobacco was used mainly in
the form of pipe tobacco, cigars, chewing tobacco, and
snuff. Although the cigarette industry really began in the
1870s when a cigarette manufacturing machine was developed, cigarettes did not become popular until World
War I. In 1914 four billion cigarettes were manufactured
in the United States. Over the years the consumption of
cigarettes has increased steadily. Today cigarette manufacture is more than 580 billion annually:

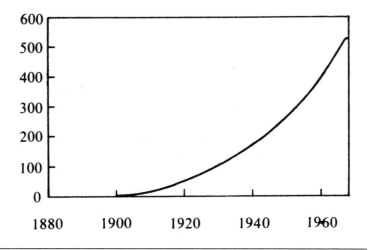

Production of cigarettes: 1900–1968

FROM RESEARCH TO REALITY: SMOKING AND HEALTH

During the years following World War II, it became evident that something was happening to the health of the
nation. Although the death rate from infectious diseases
declined, deaths from lung cancer increased.

Statistics for the year 1960 showed that 86 percent of the lung cancer deaths were among men. Between 1935 and 1960 there was a 600 percent increase in the number of lung cancer deaths among men and a 125 percent increase among women. In 1970, of 65,168 deaths from lung cancer, 81 percent were men and 19 percent were women. Statistics from the American Cancer Society indicate that the number of lung cancer deaths of adult smokers who have not smoked for ten years is very close to the number among nonsmokers.

Among young people, the number of girls under nineteen who were regular cigarette smokers went from 15 percent in 1974 to 13 percent in 1979. The number of teenage boys who smoked cigarettes went from 16 percent in 1974 to 11 percent in 1979.

Year	Number of deaths from lung cancer
1935	4,000
1945	11,000
1960	36,000
1970	65,168
1978	95,086
1982 (estimated)	111,000

Deaths from lung cancer in 1970. In the 1970s the percentage of women dying from cancer increased markedly.

In response to these statistics, four health agencies, the American Cancer Society, the American Heart Association, the American Public Health Association, and the National Tuberculosis and Respiratory Disease Association, asked President John F. Kennedy (in 1961) to appoint a commission to study the relationship of cigarette-smoking to lung cancer. The Surgeon General of the United States was empowered to assemble a panel of experts to study the problem. This Advisory Committee (consisting of ten experts acceptable to the American tobacco industry) spent more than a year reviewing all the research that had been carried on up to that time.

Over the years the evidence gathered in independent research projects pointed to the possibility that tobacco use produces harmful effects. The first well-documented clinical study of cancer was prepared by a little-known French physician, M. Bouisson.

In 1859 he wrote about sixty-eight patients whom he observed in the Montpellier Hospital. All of these patients suffered from cancer of the oral cavity: forty-five had cancer of the lip, eleven had cancer of the mouth, seven cancer of the tongue. Sixty-six of these patients smoked pipes, and one chewed tobacco. Bouisson noted that lip cancer developed at the site where pipes were held in the mouth. All of these patients smoked short-stemmed pipes (called lip burners). He concluded that the cancer resulted from irritation of the tissue by tobacco products. Bouisson suggested that long-stemmed clay pipes with non-heat-conducting materials are safer. This study went unnoticed.

Research knowledge accumulates over long periods of time before someone or some group is motivated to put it all together. The concise timetable of research studies that follows shows that investigations concerning tobacco and health had been taking place for many years.

1928:   Buerger's disease was described. It is a circu-
        latory disease that affects the arteries in the
        legs and feet. It was known to occur among
        smokers and to subside when the patient
        stopped smoking.

1936:   Surgeons Dr. Alton Ochsner and Dr. Michael
        E. DeBakey noted that all of their lung-cancer
        patients were cigarette smokers.

1938:   Dr. Raymond Pearl, a medical statistician at
        Johns Hopkins University, did a monumental
        study showing that smokers have a far shorter
        life expectancy than nonsmokers.

1939:   Dr. A.H. Roffo, an Argentinian research
        worker, induced cancer by painting tobacco
        extracts on the backs of rabbits.

1940:   Drs. John P. English, Frederick A. Willius,
        and Joseph Berkson stated that there is a
        relationship between smoking and coronary
        artery disease.

1951–   Dr. Richard Doll and Dr. A. Bradford Hill,
1956:   British investigators, showed the relationship
        between death and the number of cigarettes
        smoked per day.

1951–   Dr. E. Cuyler Hammond and Dr. Daniel
1957:   Horn performed a massive research study that
        proved conclusively that there is a relationship
        between cigarette-smoking, coronary artery
        disease, lung cancer, and general health.

1959:   Dr. Harold Dorn showed how cigarette-
        smoking affects the general health of the
        smoker.

The foregoing chronology is too brief to do justice to the
kind of intensive and extensive work that was carried out

by medical investigators seeking to determine if there was a link between cigarette-smoking and health. Perhaps you can get a better idea of the magnitude of this work from a little more detail.

The kind of study dealing with a living population is called a *prospective* study. Large teams of trained investigators kept track of a total of 1,123,000 men in seven different research projects during periods of time ranging from 44 months to 10 years. Of the total number of persons who were being studied, 65,023 died while the projects were in progress. The population included 34,000 British doctors, 188,000 men in nine states, 248,000 U.S. veterans, 67,000 industrial workers in California, 60,000 American Legion members in California, 78,000 Canadian veterans and dependents, and 448,000 men in 25 states.

Are these numbers large enough to provide valid results?

In addition to the prospective studies reports, other kinds of scientific evidence were used by the Surgeon General's Advisory Committee. These were the findings of: retrospective studies in which 36,000 death certificates and autopsy reports were studied and families of the deceased were questioned for the specifics of the illnesses; animal experiments; clinical hospital records; and statistical relationships applying to individuals and groups that helped to round out the story of smoking and health. Using all of the available evidence, the Advisory Committee concluded that:

Cigarette smoking is a health hazard of sufficient importance in the United States to warrant appropriate remedial action.

The significance of the Advisory Committee report is summarized below.

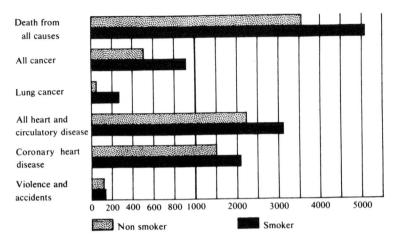

The death rate rose progressively with increasing number of cigarettes smoked per day. If a person smoked two or more packs a day, the death rate was two and a half times higher.

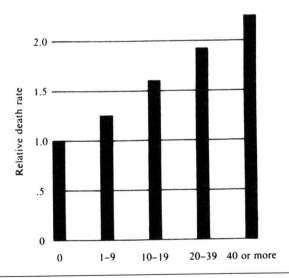

Number of cigarettes smoked per day

(Hammond Study)

- 52.1 percent of the deaths resulted from coronary artery disease.
- 13.5 percent of the deaths resulted from lung cancer.
- Lung cancer is extremely rare in nonsmokers.

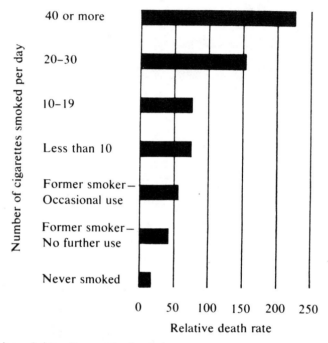

Number of cigarettes smoked per day

Relationship of lung cancer to number of cigarettes smoked per day. (Adapted from Hammond and Horn Study.)

Other diseases associated with smoking are

Gastric and duodenal ulcer
Diseases of the arteries
Lung infections
Cancer of the bladder
Cirrhosis (cancer) of the liver

Life expectancy is shortened 8.3 years for heavy smokers.

WHERE THERE'S SMOKE—THERE'S DANGER

When a cigarette is lit, this is what happens. The oxygen in the air permits the burning of the tobacco and the cigarette paper. Wherever there is burning, smoke and ash are produced. The cigarette ash is knocked off onto the ground (or into an ashtray), and although it is a little nuisance, it does not affect the health of the smoker.

But where there is smoke, there is marked danger to health. Each time a person inhales the smoke from a cigarette, certain changes go on in his body. The smoke passes from his mouth through the throat into his windpipe, through the bronchi and bronchioles, and finally into the lungs. Think of all the organs of respiration that the smoke touches.

What is this smoke that smokers so eagerly draw into their lungs? Simply stated, smoke is a mixture of nicotine, gases, and solid particles (tars). However, an analysis of the smoke components shows that the compounds that make up this mixture are not so simple.

First, let us become acquainted with the gaseous compounds in smoke.

Gaseous components	Effect
Inorganic gases	
Carbon dioxide	No effect
Carbon monoxide	Reduces the oxygen-carrying capacity of the blood; poisonous
Ammonia	Tissue irritant
Hydrogen sulfide	Tissue irritant

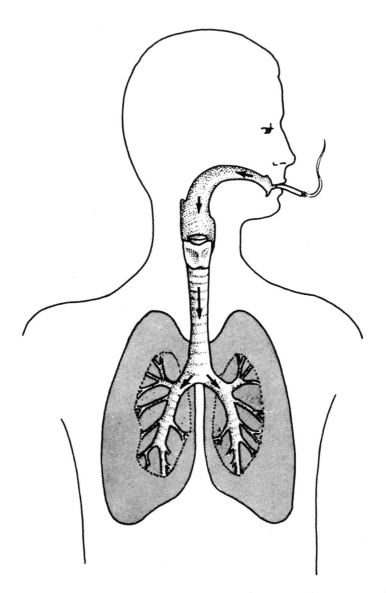

How many organs of respiration does inhaled cigarette smoke touch?

Hydrogen cyanide	Poison
Organic compounds	
Alcohols	Minor irritants
Phenols	Active cancer-producing substances
Aldehydes	Throat irritants
Benzopyrene and other aromatic polycyclic hydrocarbons	Cancer-producing substances
Others	
Arsenic	Poison; used as insecticide on tobacco leaves; filters out in the smoke

Second, let us turn our attention to the nicotine in cigarette smoke. Nicotine is an alkaloid, a drug that occurs naturally in the tobacco plant. Where have you heard the term alkaloid before? In large amounts, nicotine is a poison. If 50 to 60 milligrams (mg) of the pure drug were injected into the blood of a person, it would cause death by paralyzing the muscles of his respiratory system. In effect, the person would suffocate.

Each cigarette contains about 17 mg of nicotine. About 3 mg of the drug enters the mouth in the smoke and travels into the lungs. The capillaries surrounding the lung air sacs absorb the nicotine into the bloodstream. A smoker who uses a package of cigarettes a day absorbs about 60 mg of nicotine throughout the twenty-four-hour period. Heavy smokers take in 100 mg or more per day. If nicotine is such a potent poison, why doesn't it kill a heavy smoker?

In the first place, 10 percent of the nicotine that enters the bloodstream as a cigarette is smoked is carried directly to the kidneys. These organs filter the nicotine out of the blood into the bladder, where it leaves the body through the urine. The other 90 percent of the nicotine is transported to the liver, where it is changed chemically into a harmless state. Second, heavy smokers develop a tissue tolerance to nicotine (just as an addict does to the alkaloids in opium) and withstand increasing amounts. A person whose cigarette habit spirals to two or more packages a day is most definitely addicted to the nicotine in tobacco.

Even in heavy smokers nicotine, while circulating in the bloodstream, does harm to the organs that it passes. Nicotine:

- Affects the nerve ganglia at the junction of nerve and muscle. It stimulates then quickly depresses nerve activity. This leads to tremors and unsteadiness. (Have you ever noticed the shaking hands of heavy smokers?)
- Enlarges the pupil of the eye. It diminishes eye reflexes for strong light and near vision.
- Reduces the secretions of the stomach and the mouth. (No wonder smokers complain of "dry mouth.")
- Decreases the activity of muscles in the walls of the stomach and the intestines, leading to constipation and digestive tract difficulties.
- Stimulates the development of peptic and duodenal ulcer.
- Speeds up the rate of heartbeat, sometimes to 90 beats per minute.
- Increases the blood pressure.
- Constricts the capillaries in the hands and feet, resulting in a temporary loss of temperature.
- Decreases the activity of the urinary bladder by depressing the pituitary gland and the nerves that feed the bladder.

- Inhibits the sensitivity of the taste buds; dulls perception of subtle flavors.

Nicotine touches and influences practically every system in the body. At this time, the effect of nicotine on the reproductive system is not known. It is known that women who smoke during pregnancy have a higher rate of miscarriage and have smaller babies than do nonsmokers. However, the factor in tobacco that causes pregnancy difficulties has not been identified.

Earlier it was stated that tobacco smoke contains gases,

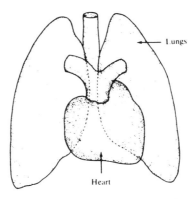

Blood from the heart's right ventricle is pumped into the lungs.

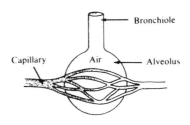

Each air sac (alveolus) is surrounded by a capillary where exchange of gases takes place. Redrawn after A. Sway—National Tuberculosis and Respiratory Disease Association.

nicotine, and solid particles. Let us find out now what happens to the solid particles in smoke. When a smoker inhales, the solid material travels through the respiratory organs. These specks stick to the moist membranes that line the bronchi, the bronchioles, and the lungs. Each time smoke is drawn into the respiratory tract, more of these solid particles are deposited on the epithelial linings. Moisture from the lungs converts the solid material into sticky tars. ("Tars" is used in the plural to show that chemically different substances are formed.) As each puff of a cigarette is taken, more of these dark tars are formed until the lungs are thickly coated by the gummy mess. After several years the lungs of regular smokers are quite black. The deposit of tars on the lung linings leads to a clogging of the air sacs. These and the capillaries that surround them are often ruptured by coughing. The heart must then pump blood through a smaller number of capillaries. Therefore, the heart works against increased pressure (because of fewer capillaries) and decreased oxygen supply (caused by destroyed air sacs.)

LUNG CANCER—PICTURE STORY

As smoke with its gases, nicotine, and tars sweeps over the lungs, changes take place in the cells of the epithelial linings. The drawings below tell the story.

Normal epithelial linings of the lungs look like this. Tall cilated cells sweep away dust particles. Rounded goblet cells secrete mucus. Nicotine and tars immobilize the cilia.

Note how the number of basal cells has increased. Carcinogens in the smoke stimulate the abnormal growth of basal cells. Have the goblet cells changed in any way?

What has happened to the ciliated, columnar epithelial cells? They and the goblet cells have become flattened.

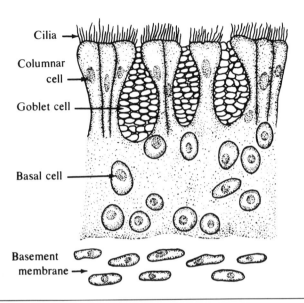

Cilia

Columnar cell

Goblet cell

Basal cell

Basement membrane

Epithelial lining of the normal lung.

Wild growth of the basal cells continues. Their nuclei are abnormal.

This is the beginning of cancer in the lung. It starts in one place. How do the cells differ in shape and position from the normal?

Then the cancer cells begin to migrate. They break through the basement membrane and spread to other parts

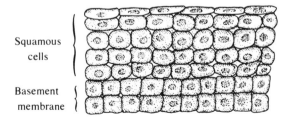

Squamous cells

Basement membrane

Epithelial lining of the lung of heavy smoker.

Goblet cell

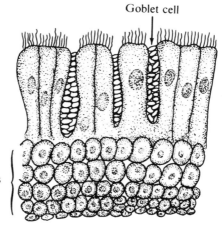

Basal cells

Note the changes that have taken place in lung tissue.

of the lung—and then to other parts of the body.

Is smoking worth this?

A WORD ABOUT "SAFE" CIGARETTES

"I am a fatalist," said Clara. "What will be, will be. Let me tell you," she continued while rummaging through her handbag, "when your number is up, that's it. You're finished. I had a sister, a saint she was, never touched a cigarette or took a drop of alcohol. At the age of twenty-three her life was over. One bout of pneumonia finished her." As Clara found the object of her search, she declared mournfully, "Only the good die young." She then carefully fitted her cigarette into the special holder, designed to filter out the nicotine and tars.

Around 1954 cigarette manufacturing companies began a mad scramble to produce the "safe" cigarette. News of the relationship of smoking to lung cancer began to seep through the news media. Many sensible people became frightened and stopped smoking. There was a noticeable dip in cigarette sales.

To recapture the shrinking market, cigarette companies developed new kinds of cigarettes. Thus began the era of king-size, filter-tip, and denicotinized cigarettes.

The greater length of the king-size cigarette (85 mm instead of the standard 70 mm) is supposed to filter the smoke as it travels from the burning tip to the mouth. "Increased mildness" was the slogan for a certain brand of cigarette. Up to certain point, the longer cigarette does filter out the tars, which are trapped on the unburned portion of the tobacco. But as this section becomes ignited, the tars are reburned and inhaled. A king-size cigarette offers some filtration possibilities as long as it is smoked only half way. But if the smoker follows the ads and "enjoys a 21 percent longer smoke," he is taking in far more tars and nicotine than in a standard-size cigarette. (Does the 100 mm cigarette filter any better?)

The filter-tip cigarette not only recaptured the shrinking cigarette market, but made it boom beyond all expectations. Cigarette advertising became more and more reckless and misleading, giving the impression that filters on cigarettes render the smoke harmless.

This is the filter-tip story. Filters, placed at one end of a cigarette, are made of paper, cotton, or cellulose. They are designed to trap nicotine, tars, and loose tobacco as the smoke passes through the filter on the way to the mouth. When a filter is efficient, trapping a high percentage of the nicotine and tars, the smoker gets no taste. Therefore, to prevent the "flat" cigarette, the manufacturers make the pores in the filters large enough to permit the passage of some nicotine and tars.

In addition, it was discovered that by using coarser tobacco (the stems and tough leaves that were once discarded) taste is returned to the filter-tip cigarette along with the tars and nicotine. The filter at the tip of the cigarette is really a gimmick designed to deceive the smoker into thinking that he has a "safer" cigarette than the standard one. There is no cigarette taste without tars and nicotine. Those are the taste factors. A study of the filter-tip cigarettes of three companies showed that their products were real health hazards.

Compared to a standard cigarette:

Brand A had 5 percent more tar and 7 percent less nicotine.

Brand B had 15 percent more tar and 33 percent more nicotine.

Brand C had 18 percent more tar and 29 percent more nicotine.

Detachable filters of all kinds increased in sales during the 1970s. There were the detachable reusables as well as the detachable disposables. These have only psychological value for the smoker. They do no better job of filtering and preserving taste.

The denicotinized cigarette is another innovation, which reduces the nicotine content by 50 percent. However, a person addicted to nicotine will smoke twice as many of those to get the same quantity of nicotine that his system requires. Another interesting fact is that low-nicotine cigarettes are made from a variety of tobacco that has low nicotine content. But the tar content is 50 percent higher. Is this advantageous to the smoker?

NICOTINE AND ADDICTION

The report on smoking by then Surgeon General C. Everett Koop indicates that the nicotine in tobacco products may be highly addictive. Regardless of the form of tobacco that people use, the results seem to be the same. Nicotine remains in the blood for twenty-four hours, so that daily tobacco users are always exposed to the effects of nicotine.

Nicotine that enters the bloodstream is rapidly transported to the brain, where it readily crosses the blood-brain barrier and accumulates in brain cells. There nicotine stimulates the cortex (outer layer of brain cells) and affects the central nervous system.

Tolerance to nicotine develops so that repeated use lessens the effects and the user increases intake. That is why so many cigarette users smoke two or more packs a day.

Breaking the smoking habit is not easy. Heavy users of cigarettes undergo withdrawal symptoms. However, tobacco dependence can be treated successfully if the user is determined to stop.

LET'S GET IT ALL TOGETHER:
A SUMMARY

1. There is a direct correlation between the number of cigarettes smoked per day and the death rate from all causes.
2. Death from all causes is higher in cigarette smokers than in nonsmokers.

3. The main killers of heavy smokers are
   (a) coronary artery disease
   (b) lung cancer
   (c) emphysema and chronic bronchitis.
4. For cigar and pipe smokers the death rates are high for
   (a) cancer of the mouth
   (b) cancer of the esophagus
   (c) cancer of the larynx
   (d) cancer of the lip.
5. Lung cancer in women is on the increase since their cigarette consumption has increased.
6. At the present trend in smoking, it is estimated that ONE MILLION of today's teenagers will die from lung cancer during adulthood. If a young person begins to smoke at the age of fourteen, and it takes twenty to twenty-five years of continuous smoking to develop lung cancer, how long is his expected life span? (Many smokers who died of coronary artery disease had cancerous spots in their lungs.)
7. IF YOU DON'T SMOKE, DON'T START. IF YOU DO, STOP!

CHAPTER 12

Caffeine: The Quick
"Picker-upper"

C offee beans, tea leaves, kola nuts, and cocoa beans contain the alkaloid caffeine. You know that an alkaloid is a chemical that contains nitrogen and is produced by plants. All alkaloids have an effect on the physiology (working) of the body. Caffeine, too, affects the body, its cells, tissues, and organs.

When isolated from other plant products, caffeine is a white, crystalline substance with a bitter taste. Ten grams of pure caffeine taken by mouth is a powerful killer. However, the small amount of caffeine in coffee, tea, cocoa, or cola acts as a mild stimulant of the central nervous system and other body organs. In fact, coffee is the favorite breakfast drink of Americans because its caffeine provides the perking up that many folks need to get going in the morning. The fact of the matter is that caffeine is a drug that arouses the brain and spinal cord.

HOW CAFFEINE AFFECTS THE BODY

Most coffee drinkers start the day with two cups of coffee. That means that they take in 150 to 300 milligrams of caffeine at one sitting. Fifteen to thirty minutes after consumption, that caffeine has measurable effects on the body: an increase in heart rate and blood pressure, elevation of the body temperature, and an increase in breathing rate. The body processes quicken, accompanied by an increase in the speed with which the body reacts to stimuli. Caffeine stimulates the gastric glands that line the stomach wall, thus increasing the flow of acid in the stomach. That is why coffee is removed from the diet of persons with ulcers. Caffeine stimulates the kidney tubules and thus increases urine production. However, caffeine has a negative effect on body cells, decreasingly their ability to oxidize sugar. The result is that blood sugar levels may rise, a fact important to diabetics.

The three major parts of the brain, the cerebrum, cerebellum, and medulla, respond to the presence of caffeine in the blood. Thinking, sensory interpretation, and voluntary movement are controlled by the cerebral cortex. Many people say that the caffeine in coffee stimulates their thought processes and helps them to be productive and creative; when they feel tired and slightly depressed, caffeine gives them a lift.

In some instances the motor skills of people improve after they have had two or three cups of coffee. A study done among typists indicated that they were able to type faster after having coffee. Some even performed above their normal level. In another study, when given the equivalent of the caffeine in two cups of coffee, bicyclists seemed to travel farther without fatigue.

The brain stem (medulla) controls involuntary activity

such as heartbeat, respiration, and movement of the involuntary muscles that make up the internal body organs and systems. Caffeine does increase the rate of heartbeat, breathing, kidney function, and the like and stimulate the flow of gastric juice in the stomach.

Any chemical that affects the physiology of the body is a drug. Caffeine is a drug that has some beneficial effects but also puts body functions at a disadvantage. Its ability to increase alertness may be detrimental. A cup of coffee taken in the evening may stimulate the brain centers so much that some people cannot sleep at night. Having rested poorly at night, they get up feeling groggy and dull. To feel better, they drink two or three cups of coffee and become more alert. As they slow down in the afternoon, they may drink more coffee. The pattern of overstimulation at night and its consequent sleeplessness continues.

People perked up by morning coffee may feel quite fatigued in the afternoon as the effects of the caffeine wear off. Caffeine has a half-life in the body of four hours. At the end of eight hours all the caffeine taken in at morning has left the body. The lows that some people feel in midafternoon may be due to the loss of caffeine and its stimulation.

Caffeine can cause overstimulation of the nervous system. Physicians recommend that people limit their coffee drinking to no more than three cups a day. Reducing the daily intake of caffeine prevents overactivation of the brain centers at night and also overexcitation of the nervous system in the day. Headache, nervousness, irritability, restlessness, and "on-edge" feelings may be signs of a nervous system overloaded with caffeine.

SOURCES OF CAFFEINE

Coffee is an important beverage in the American diet. In fact, the total consumption of coffee in the United States is two billion pounds a year. Statistics show that four out of five adults consume 3.2 cups of coffee each day. Thus, coffee is the largest single source of caffeine for millions of adults.

Tea contains caffeine, but half as much as that in coffee. Cocoa and chocolate are other sources of caffeine. You may have heard an older person say that the doctor has advised against the consuming of cola drinks. Cola drinks made from the kola nut contain caffeine, but the amount is not very significant. Some manufacturers add caffeine to cola drinks to perk up the flavor. It is estimated that the average American drinks almost 400 12-ounce servings of soft drinks a year. Two million pounds of caffeine are used as a flavor enhancer in the manufacture of soft drinks. Caffeine is added to other foods as well: powdered and prepared puddings, gelatin powders, baked goods, frozen dairy foods, and soft candy.

Caffeine is also used as an ingredient in medicines. Headache remedies such as aspirin products have caffeine added to them. Caffeine helps to reduce the size of the enlarged blood vessels in the brain that cause headache. It also serves as a mild stimulant to relieve the tired and depressed feelings that accompany headache. Other medicines that contain caffeine are cold preparations, painkillers, cough medicines, nasal and chest decongestants, allergy medicines, and preparations for premenstrual cramps. Caffeine does not relieve all of these disorders, but it gives the sufferer an energizing lift.

144 ◇   COPING WITH DRUG ABUSE

THE DANGERS OF CAFFEINE

The amounts of caffeine present in coffee, tea, and other beverages and prepared foods are not enough to cause death. However, a person who consumes too much of the alkaloid can become affected by a condition known as *caffeinism*. Caffeinism constitutes a series of reactions that result in headache, appetite loss, weight loss, frequent loose stool or diarrhea, stomach upset, rapid and shallow breathing, shaky hands, irregular heartbeat, ringing in the ears, and inability to sleep soundly.

It is not unusual for those who consume too much caffeine to experience changes in mood. They may feel irritable and anxious, fall into depression, and become excessively concerned about themselves. Loss of job efficiency may be traced to excessive consumption of coffee and other drinks containing caffeine. Some clinicians believe that hyperactivity and learning and behavior problems in school children may be due to overconsumption of

Amounts of Caffeine in Beverages and Medicines

Item	Serving/Dose	Amount of Caffeine
Regular ground coffee	6 oz	75–150 mg
Instant powdered coffee	6 oz	50–120 mg
Decaffeinated coffee	6 oz	2–5 mg
Regular tea	6 oz	35–95 mg
Instant tea	6 oz	30–140 mg
Cocoa beverage	6 oz	5–40 mg
Cola soft drink	6 oz	15–35 mg
Noncola soft drink	6 oz	15–35 mg
Cold medicine	per dose	15–30 mg
Stay-awake preparations	per dose	100–200 mg
Appetite suppressants	per dose	100–200 mg
Headache medicines	per dose	30–65 mg
Chocolate bar	1 oz	20–25 mg

caffeine in soft drinks and prepared foods. Physicians recommend that caffeine intake be limited. A safe level for daily consumption is no more than 200 milligrams. The table that follows shows the amounts of caffeine found in common beverages and medicines.

DECAFFEINATED COFFEE

In an effort to decrease their intake of caffeine, many people have turned to decaffeinated coffee. Although decaffeinated coffee contains a greatly reduced amount of caffeine, it presents another problem: Chemicals are used to remove the caffeine from the coffee bean. Although manufacturers make a conscientious attempt to remove these chemicals, some of them still remain in the beans, and users of decaffeinated coffee drink the chemicals along with the coffee. Formerly, one of the chemicals used in removing caffeine from coffee beans was trichloroethylene, a substance found to cause cancer in laboratory rats. In recent years, pure water is used to separate caffeine from coffee. Although this method is more costly, it is safer than the use of chemicals.

CAFFEINE AND ALCOHOL

A popular belief is that a cup of strong, black coffee will reverse the effects of alcohol. Actually, alcohol is a depressant that ultimately makes the person who has overindulged sleepy. Removal of alcohol from the blood is the only method of sobering up a person. When coffee is given to a person who has drunk too much alcohol, the coffee stimulates the brain centers and rouses the person. Instead of having reversed the effects of the alcohol, the coffee has stimulated the drunken person. This is very dangerous.

A person with too much alcohol in the blood becomes energized but retains the alcoholic irresponsibility, perhaps doing foolish and dangerous things such as driving a car or becoming overaggressive. It is better to let a drunken person sleep.

CAFFEINE AND PREGNANCY

Of recent years, much attention has been given to the health care of the pregnant mother and the developing fetus. Research is inconclusive about the effect of mild doses of caffeine on the fetus. However, physicians advise pregnant women to limit or stop caffeine intake during pregnancy. It has been found that miscarriages increase when pregnant women drink eight or more cups of coffee a day.

SUMMARY

Coffee drinkers may not like to think so, but caffeine is a drug. An alkaloid that has the ability to stimulate the central nervous system and affect a person's mood is classified as a drug. However, caffeine is a mild energizer and one that is socially accepted. Dangers to health accompany overstimulation by caffeine, but these can be avoided by reducing caffeine intake. It is wise to remember that caffeine is put into soft drinks, prepared foods, and medicines either for its flavor-enhancing quality or for its ability to energize. Coffee is not the only source of caffeine.

CHAPTER 13

Toward Coping
With Drug Abuse

The indiscriminate use of drugs disorders one's life. Drug abuse creates personal, social, and health problems of such enormity that to undo the damage is often quite impossible. Unfortunately, the stress of drug abuse does not remain confined to the abuser. Drug abuse is the kind of trouble that erupts from the offender and snipes at society.

As told by a high school teacher, the story of a teenage abuser illustrates the effect of drug-induced behavior, not only on the abuser, but also on those who were just casually acquainted with her.

> I was pleased to see Sylvie today. Her hair is cut short and styled nicely; her dress, appropriate to the occasion. Although her face and arms still bear some of the telltale scars, she looks pleasant enough.

Four years ago, I was not pleased to see Sylvie. Then, she was frightening and unpredictable. Some days she roamed around the classroom threatening anyone who looked at her. At other times, she fell into a deep sleep, not even awakening at the sound of the bell. Nobody dared to disturb her for fear that she might fly into a rage, unleashing threatened violence.

One day it finally happened. Sylvie lost all control—"flipped out," went berserk and wild. Running through the school corridors screaming and raging, she punched through the glass in a door, cutting herself terribly, before being subdued.

Sylvie was on drugs, reportedly Quaaludes. Over a period of four months, one could see the disintegrating personality. Extreme restlessnes, moods that changed from anger to fear to silliness, faulty vision, and other aberrant patterns of behavior were definite indicators that something was wrong.

Although Sylvie visited the school today, all is not right with her. She admits to being fearful and somewhat depressed. At odd moments flashbacks occur that drain her emotionally. In order to pay for her treatment, her parents had to sell their house. Both brothers left home, resenting the trouble that she had caused.

Sylvie's drug abuse touched the lives of many people. She lost her friends, destroyed her family, and ruined her own health. How many people had to cope with her drug abuse?

SOME SOCIAL ASPECTS OF DRUG ABUSE

An untold number of adults take legally available drugs at an astounding rate. Enormous quantities of psychoactive drugs are prescribed and dispensed for a number of psychological conditions. The reasons men and women take these drugs range from the minor frustrations of daily life to acute psychosis. Needless to say, the frequent misuse of mood-affecting drugs by adults has provided examples detrimental to the young. Television and other advertising media have reinforced the concept of drug use to avoid normal stress.

The most serious effect of drug-taking in adults is reflected in the increasing inability of parents to cope with their children. At each stage in their developing years, children require firm, loving, intelligent direction from parents. An adult whose own emotions and reactions are being controlled by drugs cannot offer proper support and guidance to young people in the household. Adults who are emotional "dropouts" raise children to follow suit.

Misuse of drugs by adults is a serious matter. Its effects can be measured by:

- The number of brain-damaged children born to alcoholic mothers.
- The number of children physically abused by a drug-abusing parent.
- The number of women who are beaten by alcoholic husbands.
- The number of persons who lose jobs because of excessive absence or inability to follow directions.
- The reduced health stamina of the drug-taking population.

• The number of drug-abusing minors who follow the example set by their parents.

THE "FUN" DRUG MYTH

Researchers from the University of Michigan's Institute for Social Research completed a study on the drug-taking habits of 18,000 high school seniors in the class of 1977. It was found that the three most widely used drugs are tobacco in the form of cigarettes, alcohol, and marijuana. Of the latter, it was noted that 26 percent of the seniors had started use in the 9th grade, while 29 percent had their first experience in the 10th grade. This indicates that more than 50 percent of the seniors were smoking pot.

Specialists in human behavior are beginning to take a more critical look at the effects of marijuana-smoking on young people. Of all the drugs with which the young are involved, marijuana has been considered the least harmful. However, scientists are beginning to express doubts as to whether marijuana is as harmless as once supposed. Any drug that affects the brain and other parts of the central nervous system is capable of doing damage.

Rod and his family moved to the city from a small Midwestern town when he was in the 9th grade. As a freshman student, he did very well scholastically. His reading ability was much above that of his classmates. In the 10th grade, Rod began smoking pot. By the time he reached the 11th grade, he was a regular user. In the 12th grade, he became a pusher so that he could get pot for nothing. Rod, the pusher, failed all of his senior subjects. He confided in a friend that he could no longer concentrate.

Surveys now indicate that extensive use of marijuana is to be found among high school students. Those who smoke it regularly have lower grades than those who do not. One large state study showed that marijuana use by high school students is associated with alcohol use, cigarette-smoking, and early dating. These cannot be construed as casual relationships, but as aspects of the social scene into which marijuana users are thrust.

Observation has been made that regular use of marijuana and other drugs seems to effect personality changes in youth. Clinicians have noted a loss of motivation, chronic lethargy, and a lack of clear-cut goals in drug-involved teenagers. The present studies do not reveal whether such personality characteristics are the direct results of marijuana (or other drugs) or whether the drugs merely magnify existent problems.

Simon will spend at least ten years of his life in a state prison. As an act of defiance against authority, he started to smoke pot in the school corridors. Soon he moved on to "uppers," then to "downers." He was "easy pickings" for the heroin pusher. As his habit grew, so did the robberies that he committed. He was given "10 to 20" for mugging. The old man whom he assaulted died.

Pat froze to death in the hallway of an abandoned building. His stepfather blamed the local high school for the boy's trouble. However, the stepfather did not mention that it was he who turned the boy out of the house in subzero weather. Neither he nor the boy's mother could cope with Pat's drug addiction.

Who, indeed, must cope with drug abuse?

A WORD ABOUT ANABOLIC STEROIDS

No doubt you have heard about athletes taking certain drugs to build up their muscles. These so-called body-building drugs are the *anabolic steroids.* Anabolic refers to body processes that build up tissues. Steroids are chemical compounds that have some similarity to cholesterol. Testosterone, a hormone produced in the male sex glands, is an anabolic steroid.

Testosterone functions in a number of ways in the body. It causes the development of male secondary sex character-istics, among which are development of bone and muscle. Testosterone not only controls hair growth but also affects emotional responses. In an adult male, the body produces from 2.5 to 10 milligrams of testosterone per day.

Some athletes misuse testosterone because of its ability to stimulate the development of muscle and increase body strength. They may take many times more than the nor-mal body production per day. Temporarily, testosterone does make an athlete perform better, but the better per-formance is short-lived. Serious side effects of the steroid may take over, among them cancer, cholesterol increase, water retention, heart disease, liver tumor, shrunken testicles, frequent urge to urinate in men, high blood pres-sure, kidney disease, and death.

The National Football League has included anabolic steroids on its list of test drugs. Other athletic leagues have followed suit. Competitors in the Olympic games are tested for the use of anabolic steroids. Positive results disqualify athletes from competition.

A slogan that has become popular in the athletic arena is "Don't lose at winning."

SOME ALTERNATIVES TO DRUG ABUSE

There are ways to prevent the start of drug use by teenagers and to curtail it once begun. Interested groups and persons (parents, teachers, church societies, and young people themselves) can work toward channeling the energies of youth into beneficial activities. It is sad to note that more times than not, parents and school authorities close their eyes to the problem of drug abuse by teenagers, recognizing that trouble exists only when situations mushroom to horrible proportions.

Said a modern Mrs. H. five years ago, "I know that Hank is only experimenting with pot." Today she does not talk about her son at all. He is confined to a mental hospital, irreversibly brain-damaged from his "experimentation" with a series of drugs.

One has only to glance at groups of teenagers as they loiter in front of schools, hang out in pizza parlors, and idle on park benches to notice that purposeful activity is missing from their lives. A casual look at their faces reveals a pathetic circumstance. A frightening number of young people today are bored, passive, and seemingly not interested in life. This kind of personal emptiness occurs because today's youth lack full development of academic and manual skills, which limits interest and initiative in pursuing worthwhile goals.

"Don't allow Amy to be idle after school," advised the teacher. Very cheerfully the parent replied, "Oh no, Amy ain't idle. At night, she hangs out in front of the sweet shop with the other kids."

Youngsters who lack motivation often associate with others who are equally bored. Together, they seek something to do, "kicks," and often decide that drugs provide an escape from boredom. It is not unusual for drug experimentation to lead to drug involvement as a way of life.

The time to help young people is before they get started on drugs. For many, involvement with drugs begins at the age of twelve or earlier. It seems logical that the home and the school have to provide alternatives to boredom and alternatives to drugs. Of course there is something better to do than to smoke (tobacco or marijuana) or to swallow pills or to consume alcohol. There must be concerted effort to develop in young people attitudes and values that oppose drugs as an acceptable means of getting through life. The point has to be made that drugs provide only temporary, counterfeit experiences, which in no way alter the real world around them. Only purposeful, constructive activity can do that.

There *are* alternatives to drug abuse. One set of alternatives is related to keeping busy and active. Sports, team activities, school clubs, community service endeavors, part-time jobs, hobbies, home chores, and projects involving neighborhood rehabilitation are some of the ways in which time can be used constructively. From their earliest years, school-age children must be taught to enjoy constructive participation. Parents, educators, and community organizations have to accept the responsibility of providing the necessary recreational, vocational, and avocational facilities and opportunities for every child.

"I am very thrifty," said Mrs. P. "I don't sling money around, and I don't let my kids toss it around, either. In fact, I make Lola share a pack of cigarettes with her brother." (Lola was fifteen years old; her brother, thirteen.)

The desire to engage in healthy, constructive activities is not inherent in youngsters and must be motivated. Contrary to popular notion, art, music, team sports, athletics, and the like are not silly and unnecessary frills, but most essential to the education of boys and girls. A community that balances its budget by wiping out programs of enrichment is actually delivering its youth into the hands of the drug pushers.

Another set of alternatives to drug abuse lies in the realm of goals and values. It is very distressing to find so many young people who are bored with school and learning and who have no career goals or vocational aspirations. They drift from class to class learning nothing. They flounder in this rapidly changing social and cultural climate. They are devoid of values by which to live and lack specific goals to pursue. The school has fallen down on the job of providing leadership through which these young people can become involved in pursuits of positive living.

Engaging in team sports is a healthy and constructive activity.

An interest in the outdoors is a healthy and enriching activity.

Parents and educators must take a more realistic view of the needs of young people in their care and make decided efforts to enhance the quality of life. The money spent on drug rehabilitation programs, hospital care for the drug abusers, and prisons for those caught committing drug-related crimes might be better spent in enrichment programs designed to prevent drug abuse by directing the young into pathways of positive living.

SUMMARY

Boys and girls are curious and idealistic. The curiosity can be subverted into deviant behavior if not channeled correctly; the idealism, tarnished. Poor examples set by parents and other adults in authority coupled with societal negligence fosters drug abuse in the young. There are reasonable alternatives to drug abuse which, if followed, will improve the quality of our young people's lives.

Glossary

addictive   causing tissue tolerance; physical dependency; craving.

alcohol   an organic derivative of grain, fruit, or wood resulting from fermentation.

alcoholic   person addicted to alcohol.

alkaloid   drug derivatives of plants.

amphetamine   family of synthetic stimulants.

analgesic   drug that masks the ability to feel pain.

anesthetic   drug that numbs an organ or reduces the sense of pain.

antibiotic   drug produced by molds or other fungous plants that can inhibit the growth of bacteria.

ATP   adenosine triphosphate, a molecule that stores cellular energy.

barbiturates   synthetic depressants that cause tissue tolerance.

Benzedrine   member of the amphetamine family; drug used in nasal sprays.

biochemical   involving chemical reactions of cells, tissues, and organs.

cancer   abnormal growth of cells.

caffeine   mild stimulant found in coffee beans, tea leaves, kola nuts, and cocoa beans.

Cannabis sativa   species name of the hemp plant that produces marijuana.

cell   unit of structure and function of living things.

cerebral cortex   layer of gray matter in the cerebrum rich in synapses.

cerebrum   largest part of the brain in mammals; center of thought, memory, and higher processes.

chromosomes   structures in the nucleus that carry hereditary traits.

cocaine   a white powdery or crystalline drug used to elevate the mood; causes delusions in the user.

crack   cocaine altered to a form that can be smoked.

delirium tremens   hallucinatory episode brought on by alcoholism.

delusions   false, persistent belief or opinion not substantiated by evidence.

denatured alcohol   alcohol to which poisonous substances have been added to make it unfit for drinking.

depressant   drug that depresses the activity of the medulla oblongata.

dilate   to open.

drug dependency   inability to do without a particular drug.

economic   relating to management of income.

emotional   pertaining to the emotions.

Erythroxylon coca   coca tree; source of cocaine.

euphoria   light-headed giddiness; a "high."

fetal alcohol syndrome   series of defects found in babies of alcoholic women.

flashback   condition in which an LSD trip recurs weeks or months after a person has consumed the drug.

ganga   Indian name for marijuana.

hallucination   the perception of sights and sounds that are not present.

hallucinogen   drug that causes hallucinations.

hashish   strong variety of Cannabis.

heroin   narcotic drug made by altering morphine.

high   state of euphoria; giddiness; intoxication.

hyperactive abnormally active.

hypothalamus part of the forebrain near the cerebrum that controls emotions and body temperature.

ice smokable form of methamphetamine; very addictive.

illicit drugs illegal drugs.

ingestion intake of food.

intoxicated drunk; "high"; insensible.

joint dried crushed marijuana rolled in paper for smoking.

LSD shortened term for d-lysergic acid diethylamide.

mainline to inject drugs into the veins.

medicine drug or other substance used to treat disease.

methadone synthetic narcotic that resembles opium in chemical structure, used as a substitute for heroin.

methamphetamine member of the amphetamine family, also known as methedrine, Desoxyn, speed.

methaqualone a hypnotic sedative.

Miltown synthetic depressant; trade name.

mitigate to make less severe.

morphine narcotic drug obtained from the opium poppy.

Nicotiana rustica wild species of tobacco.

Nicotiana tabacum species of tobacco plant that is used for commercial tobacco.

opium narcotic drug obtained from the unripe seed pods of the opium poppy.

paranoia psychological disorder characterized by delusions of grandeur or persecution.

pep pills amphetamines, used to elevate the mood.

pharmacologist scientist who specializes in the study of drugs (medicines).

phencyclidine (PCP) anesthetic that causes hallucinations.

psychedelic refers to bizarre colors seen during hallucinations.

psychological of the mind.

psychopath   person with a disorganized abnormal personality; usually cruel and dangerous.

psychotic   person having a seriously disorganized personality.

pyloric sphincter   ring of muscle between the stomach and upper portion of the small intestine.

Quaalude   methaqualone, synthetic sedative; addictive.

reefer   marijuana joint.

reticular formation   sensory coordination region of the brain that extends through the medulla to the cerebral hemispheres.

roach   partially smoked marijuana joint.

sedative   depressant of the central nervous system.

snort   to draw in drugs, such as heroin or cocaine, through the nose.

skin popping   injecting drugs under the skin.

speed freak   person addicted to methamphetamine.

stimulant   drug that speeds up activities of cells.

symptom   condition that is a sign or signal of disease.

tars   solid organic particles that result from burning tobacco.

tetany   spasm (tightening) of the muscles.

tetrahydrocannabinol   (THC) substance in Cannabis that causes euphoria.

thalamus   part of the forebrain that coordinates sensory images.

tissue tolerance   condition in which body cells and tissues adjust to increasing amounts of a particular drug.

trip   mind changes through which a person goes under the influence of hallucinogenic drugs.

zymase   enzyme given off by yeast cells.

Bibliography

Ashley, Richard. *Cocaine—Its History, Uses, Effects*. St. Martin's Press, New York, N.Y. 1975.

Beattie, Melody. *Crack, the Facts*. Hazelden Educational Materials, Center City, Minn., 1989.

Bender, David L. *Chemical Dependency: Opposing Viewpoints*. Greenhaven Press, St. Paul, 1985.

Carroll, Marilyn. *Quaaludes: The Quest for Oblivion*. Chelsea House, New York, 1985.

Cashman, J. *The LSD Story*. Fawcett Publications, Greenwich, Conn., 1966.

Chauncey, H.W., and Kirpatrick, L.A. *Drugs and You*. Oxford Book Co., New York, 1969.

Cohen, Sidney. *The Drug Dilemma*. McGraw-Hill Books, New York, 1969.

Deschin, C.S. *The Teenager in a Drugged Society*. Richards Rosen Press, New York, 1972.

Deutsch. *Children of Alcoholics—Understanding and Helping*. Health Communications, Hollywood, Fla., 1983.

Etons, Ursula. *Angel Dusted—A Family's Nightmare*. Macmillan Publications, New York, 1979.

Fiddle, Seymour. *Portraits From a Shooting Gallery*. Harper and Row, New York, 1967.

Fort, Joel. *Alcohol: Our Biggest Drug Problem*. McGraw-Hill Book Co., New York, 1973.

Furst, Peter E. *Mushrooms: Psychedelic Fungi*. Chelsea House, New York, 1986.

Goldstein, R. *1 in 7: Drugs on College Campus*. Walker and Co., New York, 1966.

Gorodetzky, C.W., and Christian, S.T. *What You Should Know*

About Drugs. Harcourt, Brace, Jovanovich, New York, 1970.

Grinspoon, Lester, and Bakalar, James B. *Cocaine—A Drug and Its Social Evolution.* Basic Books, New York, 1976.

Houser, N.W. *Drugs—Facts on Their Use and Abuse,* Scott, Foresman and Co., Glenview, Ill., 1966.

Lee, Essie E. *Alcohol—Proof of What?* Julian Messner, New York, 1976.

Lindbeck, Vera. *The Woman Alcoholic.* Public Affairs Pamphlet No. 529, New York.

Linkletter, Art. *Drugs at My Doorstep.* World Books, Waco, Texas. 1973.

Marin, Peter, and Cohen, Allan Y. *Understanding Drug Use.* Harper & Row, New York, 1971.

Modell, W., and Lansing, A. *Drugs.* Life Science Library, Time/ Life Books, New York, 1967.

North, Robert, and Orange, Robert. *Teenage Drinking—The # 1 Drug Threat to Young People Today.* Macmillan Co., New York, 1980.

Plaut, Thomas F. (ed). *Alcohol Problems.* Oxford University Press, New York and London, 1967.

Resource Guide to Alcohol and Drug Abuse Services. Prepared by the Office of the Brooklyn Borough President, Brooklyn, N.Y. 11201.

Sanberg, Paul. *Over the Counter Drugs: Harmless or Hazardous.* Chelsea House, New York, 1986.

Silverstein, Alvin and Virginia. *Alcoholism.* J.B. Lippincott Co., Philadelphia, 1975.

Sonnett, Sherry. *Smoking.* Franklin Watts, New York, 1977.

Stwertka, Eve and Albert. *Marijuana.* Franklin Watts, New York, 1979.

BROCHURES

"Anabolic Steroids." DHHS Publication No. (FDA) 88-3171.

"*Cocaine Papers.*" D.I.N. Publications, Phoenix, Ariz.
"*Crack, The New Menace.*" U.S. Customs Service Drug Awareness Program.
"*Crack Down on Crack.* " Div. of Substance Abuse Services, New York State.
"*Information and Programs to Fight Drug Abuse.*" U.S. Customs Service Drug Awareness Program.
"*Marijuana—the Gateway Drug.*" U.S. Customs Service Drug Awareness Program.

Index